M3 MACBOOK AIR 2024 USER GUIDE

A Simplified Manual With Complete Step By Step Instructions For Beginners & Seniors On How To Operate The 13-Inch & 15-Inch M3 MacBook Air With Tips & Tricks

BY

TERRY HARLEY

Contents

INTRODUCTION

The MacBook Air is Apple's most popular laptop, and it's the perfect device for many individuals because it performs everyday work without stress. In March 2024, Apple released the M3 MacBook Air which is an upgrade when compared to the previous generation. Thanks to the M3 chip, the new MacBook Air has not only improved performance, but also increased energy efficiency, and a long battery life.

FEATURES OF THE M3 MACBOOK AIR

Design update

Apple didn't make any design updates to the 2024 MacBook Air. The device still has the same slim & compact design as the previous generation M2 MacBook Air. The M3 MacBook Air is available in two size options (15-inch and 13-inch), and four colour options (Space Gray, Silver, Starlight, and Midnight).

The 13-inch model is 11.30mm thick, 11.970" long, 8.460" inches deep, and weighs about 2.70 pounds. The 15" model is significantly bigger; it's 11.50mm thick, 13.40" long, and 9.350" deep and weighs about 3.30 pounds.

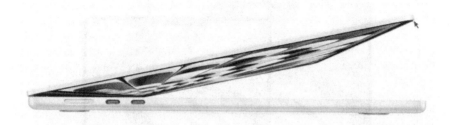

On the left side of both devices, you'll find 2 Thunderbolt/ USB-C ports, as well as a MagSafe charging port.

The M3 MacBook Air has a Touch ID fingerprint sensor close to the FN keys on the keyboard. You can use Touch ID to unlock your MacBook, authenticate purchases, sign into some 3rd-party applications, and more.

Screen

The M3 MacBook Air has thin bezels and uses "Liquid Retina display technology". The 13" model has a resolution of 2560 by 1664 at 224 pixels per inch, while the 15" model has a resolution of 2880 by 1864 at 224.0 pixels per inch. The screen offers support for a billion colours & P3 Wide colour for clear, true-to-life colours.

The M3 MacBook Air also supports True Tone, which is designed to change the colour of the screen to match room lighting.

Storage Capacity

The M3 MacBook Air has a storage capacity of up to 2TB. The base level storage begins at 256GB.

CHAPTER 1

HOW TO SETUP YOUR MACBOOK

When configuring your MacBook, you can personalize some settings, setup features like Touch ID & Apple Pay, and transfer data from another PC or Mac.

When you switch on your MacBook Air for the 1st time, the Setup Assistant will walk you through the steps you need to get started. You can answer all the prompts, or you can skip a few steps and choose to configure them later.

The Setup Assistant will guide you through the following:

→ First, you'll see Hello in different languages; simply click on the **Get Started** button to continue the setup.

→ Choose one of the languages
→ Choose your region or country: This will determine the time zone & language of your MacBook Air.

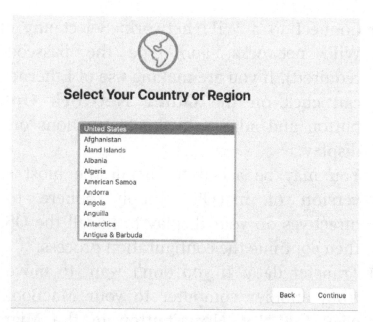

→ Enable Accessibility features: Check out the accessibility options for Cognitive, Motor, Vision, & Hearing abilities, or choose the **Not Now** option.

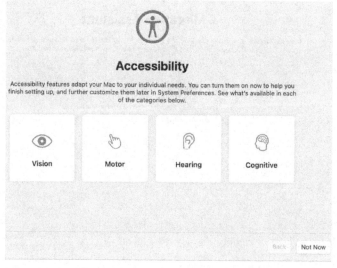

→ Connect to a WiFi network: Select any of the WiFi networks, and type the passcode (if required). If you are making use of Ethernet, you can click on the **Other Network Options** button and adhere to the instructions on your display.

You may be asked to install the most recent version of macOS. Simply adhere to the directives on your display to install the OS, and then continue the configuration process.

→ Transfer data: If you don't want to move data from another computer to your MacBook Air, click the **Not Now** button in the Migration Assistant screen.

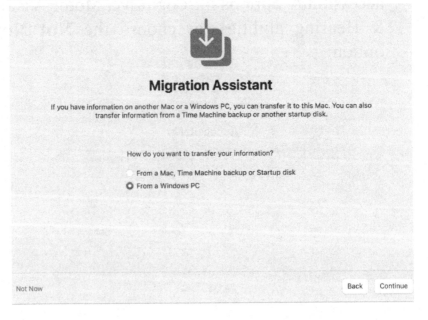

Migration Assistant

If you have information on another Mac or a Windows PC, you can transfer it to this Mac. You can also transfer information from a Time Machine backup or another startup disk.

How do you want to transfer your information?

○ From a Mac, Time Machine backup or Startup disk
◉ From a Windows PC

Not Now   Back   Continue

➔ Log in with Apple ID: An Apple ID contains an e-mail address & passcode.

Sign In with Your Apple ID

Sign in to use iCloud, iTunes, App Store, iMessage, FaceTime and more.

Set Up Later

Apple ID [Email]

Create new Apple ID...   Forgot Apple ID or password?

This Mac will be associated with your Apple ID, and data such as photos, contacts and documents will be stored in iCloud so you can access them on other devices. See how your data is managed...

Use different Apple IDs for iTunes and iCloud?

An Apple ID is an account you use for everything you do with Apple —which includes making use of iCloud, Apple Books, Apps Store, etc. If you do not have an Apple ID, you can create one for yourself while setting up your device.

➔ Create a computer account: Enter your full name, Account name, & passcode in the appropriate boxes; this info can later be used to unlock your laptop or confirm certain actions. To change your account login photo, click it, and then choose any of the available options.

Create a Computer Account

Fill out the following information to create your computer account.

Full name:

Account name:

This will be the name of your home folder.

Password: new password   verify

Hint: optional

☑ Allow my Apple ID to reset this password

Back   Continue

→ Save files in iCloud: With the iCloud feature, you can store your files in the cloud, and access them from any of your Apple Devices or the iCloud.com website; just make sure you're using one Apple ID on all your Apple devices.

→ Activate Location Services. Choose whether to allow applications like the Map app to use your MacBook Air's location. To change the settings later, click on the Apple menu icon in the upper left corner of your screen, click on System Settings in the menu, click on the **Privacy and Security** button in the sidebar on the left side of the window, and then click on Location Services & select your preferences.

→ Choose whether to share Analytics with Apple & Developers. To change the settings later, click on the Apple menu icon in the upper left corner of your screen, click on System Settings in the menu that appears, click on the **Privacy and Security** button in the sidebar on the left side of the window, click on **Analytics & Improvements** on the right side of the window and select your preferences.

→ Configure Screen Time: This feature helps you to keep track of and get reports on your laptop usage. To activate this feature, click the **Continue** button, or click on the **Setup Later** option. To configure this feature later, click the Apple menu icon in the menu bar, click on System Settings in the menu, click on the **Screen Time** button in the sidebar, and then setup the feature.

→ Use FileVault to secure your data: FileVault helps protect your data.

→ Activate Siri & Hey Siri: You can activate Siri and "Hey Siri". To setup Siri, click on the **Enable Ask Siri** button. To activate the "Hey Siri" feature, simply say a few Siri commands when asked to.

→ Setup Touch ID: You can add a fingerprint to Touch ID, which you can use to unlock your MacBook Air, authenticate purchases, sign into some 3rd-party applications, and more.

→ Setup Apple Pay: Adhere to the instructions on your display to configure Apple Pay

→ Choose your MacBook's desktop appearance: Pick Auto, Dark, or Light for your desktop look. If you want to change the option you picked, click the Apple menu icon in the menu bar, click on System Settings in the menu that appears, click on Appearance, and then select any of the options.

Charge your MacBook's battery

Your device's battery recharges anytime you connect it to power.

To charge the battery, simply use the cable & power adapter that came with your device to connect it to a power outlet.

CHAPTER 2

EXTERNAL DISPLAY, MOUSE, TRACKPAD, KEYBOARD, AND OTHER ACCESSORIES

Connect accessories to your MacBook Air

You can connect your Mac to other devices, such as a trackpad, mouse, or keyboard; wearable devices such as AirPods; & others.

Getting Started: Before connecting the device to your Mac, do the following:

- Go through the documentation that came with the accessory.
- Ensure your Mac is using the latest macOS version.
- If you're using a cable to connect your MacBook Air to the accessory, ensure you have the right cable.

Connect the wireless device

Enable Bluetooth. Click on the Control Centre icon ⬛ in the top right side of your screen. The Bluetooth icon ⍟ is blue when it is activated. If the Bluetooth icon ⍟ is gray, click the icon to enable the **Bluetooth** feature.

Pair a Bluetooth device. The 1st time you use a Bluetooth device on your Mac, you need to pair it. Go through the manual that came with the Bluetooth device to ensure it's ready for pairing—for example, you might have to press a button or flip a switch to enable the Bluetooth feature on the device. Your MacBook Air & the Bluetooth device must be switched on and close to each other.

When the Bluetooth device is ready to pair, click the Apple menu button in the top left corner of your screen, click on **Systems Settings** in the menu that pops up, and click on the **Bluetooth** button in the sidebar. Choose the Bluetooth device in the Nearby Device list, and then click the **Connect** button.

Connect a Bluetooth device. The Bluetooth device will automatically connect to your Mac after you have paired it. To view which Bluetooth devices you've connected to your MacBook, click the Control Center icon⬚ in the top right part of your display, then move the cursor over Bluetooth and click on the arrow⟩.

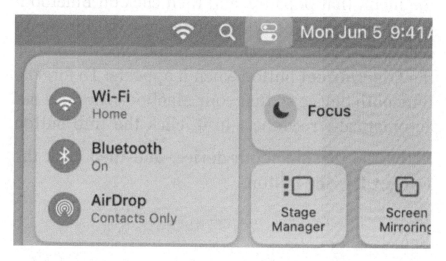

The accessories that have a blue icon in the list are connected to your MacBook Air.

If an accessory does not connect automatically, click the Apple menu button in the top left corner of your screen, click on Systems Setting in the menu that pops-up, and click on **Bluetooth** on the side bar. Ensure the Bluetooth accessory is in the **My Device** list. If you cannot find the accessory there, just adhere to the instructions above to pair it with your MacBook Air.

Disconnect or forget a Bluetooth device. To disconnect a Bluetooth device from your MacBook Air, click the Apple menu button in the upper left corner of your screen, click on System Settings in the menu that pops-up, and then click on Bluetooth in the Sidebar. Hover the cursor over the Bluetooth accessory in the **My Device** menu, and then click the **Disconnect** button when it appears. To forget a Bluetooth device so that your MacBook Air does not automatically reconnect to it, click the Info button ⓘ beside the Bluetooth device, and then click the **Forget Device** button.

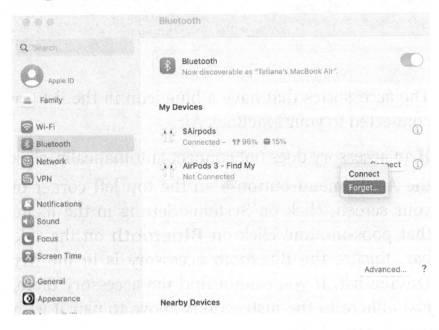

Connect a Magic Mouse, Trackpad, or Keyboard. Use the cable that came with the Magic Mouse, Trackpad, or Keyboard, to connect the accessory to your device. Then, switch on the accessory (slide the switch, ensure green is visible). The accessory will automatically pair with your MacBook Air

After the accessory pairs with your device, you can remove the cable and use it wirelessly. Your Magic Mouse, Trackpad, or Keyboard will automatically connect to your MacBook Air when Bluetooth is activated.

Use a cable to connect an accessory

You can use a cable to connect some accessories to your MacBook. If the accessory and cable/cord are capable, you might be able to move data or charge the accessory when it's connected to your MacBook.

Before connecting the accessory to your device, go through the manual that came with your accessory. Some accessories have additional power sources that must be plugged in.

To connect the accessory, you must use a cable that matches the port on the accessory as well as the port on your MacBook Air.

Magic keyboard

Your MacBook's keyboard has inbuilt features that make it easy to perform many system functions with the tap of a button; features like adding emoji, changing the keyboard language, locking your MacBook Air, and more. The Touch ID Magic Keyboard allows you to use a registered fingerprint to sign in & make purchases with Apple Pay.

Touch ID (power button)

Lock your device. Press Touch ID to lock your device. To unlock your device, open the lid and touch the **Touch ID** sensor, or press one of the keys on the keyboard and insert your passcode.

Switch on your device: Open your MacBook's lid, and then press the Power button or the Touch ID sensor.

18

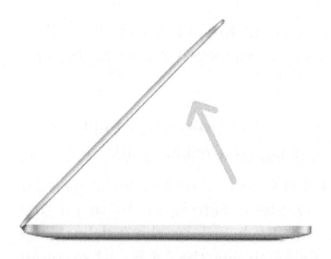

Shut down your device: To switch off your device, click on the Apple men icon in the upper part of your display, and then click on Shut Down in the menu that pops-up.

Configure Touch ID. You can use your registered fingerprint to unlock your MacBook Air and authenticate payments in many applications & sites. If you didn't setup Touch ID when setting up your MacBook Air, you can set it up any time you like in the **Touch ID and Passcode** settings in System Settings.

Use Touch ID. After setting up Touch ID, you can gently place your registered finger on the Touch ID sensor to unlock our MacBook Air. When you first turn on or restart your MacBook Air, you must enter your password to log in to your device. After that, you can use Touch ID whenever you are asked for a passcode.

Configure keyboard options: To set options for the keyboard and Function/Globe key⊕, click the Apple menu button in the top left corner of your screen, click on Systems Setting in the menu that pops-up, click on Keyboard in the sidebar, and select options for changing the keyboard or input source, displaying emoji and symbols, starting dictation, defining functions, etc.

Use symbols & emoji: Press the Globe button⊕ /Fn button on your keyboard to display the emoji picker.

Use the function keys. The function keys provide shortcuts to the following system functions:

→ Brightness (F1, F2): Press the Reduce brightness key ☼ or the Increase brightness key ☼ to decrease or increase your MacBook's screen brightness

→ Mission Control (F3): Press the Mission Control key ⊟ to see what is running on your Mac, including all spaces and open windows.

➔ Spotlight Search (F4): Press the Spotlight button $\mathbb{Q}$ to launch Spotlight and search for items on your Mac.

➔ Siri/Dictation (F5): Press the Microphone key $\underline{\mathbb{Q}}$ to enable dictation—you can dictate text in any application that allows text editing. Hold down the Microphone button $\underline{\mathbb{Q}}$ to enable Siri, and then say your request.

➔ DND (F6): Press the DND button $\mathbb{C}$ to enable or deactivate Do Not Disturb. When DND is active, you will not hear or see notifications on your Mac, but you can check the Notifications Centre to see if you have any notifications.

➔ Media (F7, F8, F9): Press the Rewind button ◁◁ to rewind, the Pause/Play button ▷|| to pause or play, or the Fast Forward button ▷▷ to fast-forward songs, movies, or slideshows.

➔ Silent (F10): Press the Silent button ◁ to mute the sound from the internal speakers.

➔ Volume (F11, F12): Press the volume down key ◁⟩ or the volume up key ◁⟩⟩⟩ to increase or reduce the volume of your MacBook.

Keyboard shortcuts

To get things done faster on your device, you can use combinations called keyboard shortcuts. A keyboard shortcut consists of a modifier key(s) (like Command (Cmd or ⌘), Shift (⇧), Alt (⌥), etc.) and another key, pressed simultaneously. For instance, hold down the Command key and then press the X key on your keyboard to cut an item

View keyboard shortcuts

Shortcuts appear beside menu items in macOS applications.

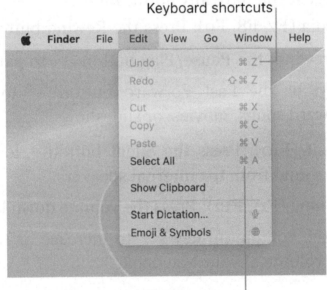

Keyboard shortcuts

Symbols represent modifier keys.

Personalize keyboard shortcuts

You can create some keyboard shortcuts by changing key combinations.

➔ Click on the Apple menu button in the upper part of your screen, click on **System Setting** in the menu that pops-up, click on Keyboard on the side bar, and click on Keyboard Shortcuts on the right part of the window.

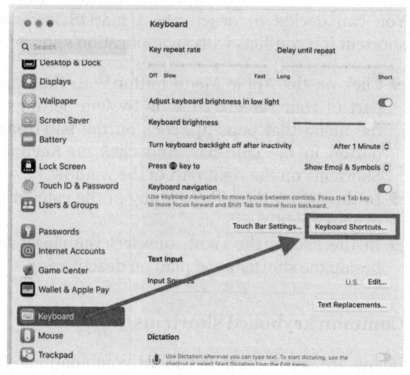

➔ In the list on the left, pick any of the categories, like Spotlight.

➔ In the list on the right, select the check box beside the shortcut you plan on changing.
➔ Double-click the current combination, then press another combination.
➔ To use the new keyboard shortcuts, quit & reopen the application you want to use the shortcut for.

Turn off a keyboard shortcut

You can decide to deactivate a macOS keyboard shortcut if it conflicts with an application's shortcut.

➔ Click on the Apple Menu button in the upper part of your screen, click on System Settings in the menu that pops-up, click on the **Keyboard** button in the side bar, and click on Keyboard Shortcuts on the right part of the window.
➔ In the list on the left, pick any of the categories, like Spotlight.
➔ In the list on the right, unselect the check box beside the shortcut you plan on deactivating.

Common keyboard shortcuts

Below are some basic keyboard combinations you can use to perform basic tasks on your MacBook Air.

→ Cmd-X: Cut the highlighted items and copy them.

→ Cmd-C: Copy the highlighted items.

→ Cmd-V: Paste the copied items in the new document or application.

→ Command-Z: Undo the last command. Press the Cmd-Shift-Z to redo the command.

→ Cmd-A: Highlight all the items.

→ Command-F: launch the search window or look for things in a doc.

→ Cmd-H: Conceal the front application window. Press the Cmd-Option-H combination to see the front application but conceal every other application

→ Cmd-M: Minimize the front window

→ Command-N: Launch a new window or doc.

→ Cmd-O: Open the highlighted items, or launch a dialog to highlight a file to open.

→ Cmd-S: Save the file.

→ Cmd-P: Print the document.

→ Command-Q: close the present application

➔ Cmd-Option-Esc: Select an application to Force Quit.

Trackpad

You can do a lot on your device with basic trackpad gestures.

Click: Press anywhere on your MacBook's track-pad. Or turn on the "Tap to click" feature in

Trackpad Settings in System Settings, so that you can perform the **Click** feature by just tapping.

Force click: Click & press deeper. With the Force-Click feature, you can find more information about something, for instance, click on a word to display the meaning of the word.

Zoom: Put 2 of your fingers on the trackpad and pinch open or closed to zoom in or out of web pages & images.

Swipe between applications: To move from one full-screen application to another, just swipe right or left on the Trackpad with 3 or 4 of your fingers.

Open Launchpad: Pinch closed with 4 or 5 fingers, then click on an application to launch it.

Two-finger scroll: Slide down or up with 2 of your fingers to scroll

Secondary/right-click: Click with 2 fingers. Or press the Control button on your keyboard & click the trackpad

Swipe to navigate: Use 2 of your fingers to swipe to the right or left on the Trackpad to flip through docs, web pages, etc.

Personalize your gestures. Select the Apple menu icon⬛ at the top of your screen, click System Setting in the menu that pops-up, and then click on Trackpad in the side bar. You can carry out the following:

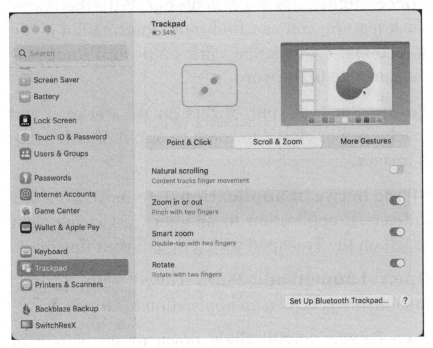

→ Get more info about gestures
→ Adjust the click pressure to the pressure you want to use
→ Adjust the speed
→ Personalize other track-pad functions
→ And more

Magic Mouse

If you decide to purchase a Magic Mouse, follow the instructions at the beginning of this chapter to pair & connect it to your MacBook Air, and adhere to the directives below to learn how to use the external Mouse (Magic Mouse).

Switch off/on: Slide the off/on switch on the mouse to switch it on (green means On).

Click: Use any of your fingers to press the upper surface of the mouse.

Secondary click (i.e., right-click): Use any of your fingers to press the right or left part of the Magic mouse (To activate left or right-click, click on the Apple Menu icon in the top of your display, click on System Settings in the menu that pops-up, click on the **Mouse** button in the sidebar, and then select "Secondary click"). Or press the Ctrl button on the keyboard while clicking the mouse.

360° Scrolling: Pan or scroll in the direction you want by brushing along the mouse surface with a finger.

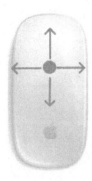

Zoom: Press & hold the Control button on your keyboard, and scroll with a finger to zoom in on things on your display.

(To activate the Zoom feature, click on the Apple Menu button in the top of your display, click on Systems Setting in the menu that pops-up, click on the **Accessibility** button, click on Zoom then choose **Use Scroll Gesture with Modifier Key to Zoom**)

Swipe with two fingers: Swipe to the right or left to surf through pictures, pages, etc.

31

Change the mouse settings. To change mouse settings like scroll speed, tracking, and more, simply click on the **Mouse** button on the sidebar in **Systems Settings**.

Watch a demo

→ To see your MacBook's trackpad gestures & a short video showing every gesture, click on the Apple Menu icon at the top of your display, click on **Systems Settings** in the menu that pops-up, and then click on the Trackpad button on the sidebar.

→ To see your MacBook's mouse gestures & a short video showing every gesture, click the Apple menu button in the top of your display, click on **Systems Settings** in the menu that pops-up, and then click on the Mouse button on the sidebar.

You can also deactivate or personalize gestures in the Mouse settings.

Charge the batteries in your accessories

The external or Magic Trackpad, Mouse, & Keyboard all have internal rechargeable batteries.

To check the battery level while they are connected to your MacBook Air, click the Control Centre icon in the upper right corner of your display, click on the Bluetooth icon , and then select the device.

To charge the battery, just use a USB-C to Lightning Cable to connect the accessory to your MacBook Air.

Drag & drop an item

You can drag and drop items on your MacBook Air.

→ On your MacBook, select the item you want to drag, like a picture or text.

➔ Hold down the trackpad or mouse while dragging the object to a different location on your display.

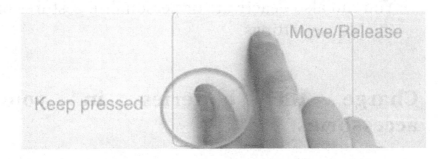

To copy the item instead of moving it, hold down the Option key on the keyboard while dragging.
➔ Release the mouse or trackpad to drop the item in another location.

External display

You can connect an external display (such as a TV, projector, etc.) to your device. The Thunderbolt/USB port on your device supports video output.

Getting started

➔ Turn on the External display before connecting it to your MacBook.
➔ Use the appropriate cable/cord for the external display: Go through the manual that came with

the external display and ensure you are using the right cable/cord to connect your device to the display.

→ See technical specifications: For more information on the type of display your MacBook is compatible with, simply click on the Apple Menu icon in the upper left corner of your display, click on the **System Settings** button in the menu that pops up, click on the **Help** button > MacBook Air Specification, and then look for Display Support (You might have to scroll).

Connect an external display to your MacBook Air

You can connect up to two different external displays to your M3 MacBook Air.

Adhere to the directives below to connect the first external display:

→ Switch on the external display
→ Use the external display's video cord/cable to connect it to your MacBook air's Thunderbolt/ USB 4 port (if needed, you can use an adapter).
→ After connecting it, your MacBook Air will automatically detect the external display

When you want to connect the 2nd display, simply adhere to the instructions below:

→ Connect an external trackpad, keyboard, or mouse to your device.

→ Close the MacBook Air's lid

→ Ensure your MacBook Air is charged (you can connect it to power if the battery is low).

→ Connect the 2nd display to power.

→ Lastly, use a cable/cord to connect the display to your MacBook Air.

After connecting the external display

Configure the external displays. After connecting an external display or projector, click on the Apple Menu icon in the upper left corner of your display, click on the **System Settings** button in the menu that pops up, and then click on the **Displays** button in the sidebar to configure the layout of the displays, pick your primary display, change the refresh rate, etc.

If you connect 2 displays to your device, the first display you connect will be the main/primary display. To change the main external display, disconnect both of them from your Mac, and then reconnect them (ensure you reconnect the primary display first).

CHAPTER 3

YOUR MACBOOK AIR

The Desktop

The desktop is the first thing you see on the MacBook Air.

Tip: Can't see the cursor on your display? To make it bigger temporarily, move one of your fingers back & forth quickly on the trackpad.

The desktop is where you open & use applications, work on files, search your device or the internet using Spotlight, etc. To change your desktop wallpaper, click on the Apple menu button in the upper part of your screen, click on **Systems Settings** in the menu that pops-up, click on the **Wallpaper** button, and choose one of the options.

Menu bar: The menus bar can be found at the upper part of your display. You can utilize the menus on the left part of the menu bar to select commands & perform tasks in applications. The items on the menu bar change depending on the application you are making use of. You can use the icons on the right corner of the menus bar to check your WiFi status , connect to a WiFi network, open the Control Centre , search with Spotlight , etc.

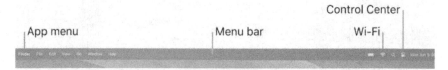

Apple menu: The Apple menu contains items you use very often and can be found in the top left edge of your display. Click on the Apple icon to launch it.

38

Apple menu

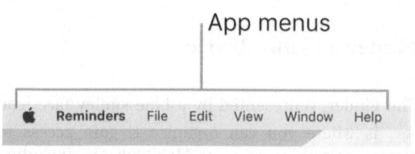

Application menu: You can have more than one window & application open at the same time. The name of the active application will be displayed in bold on the right side of the Apple menu , as well as the unique menus of that application.

App menus

If you launch another application or click on one of the open windows in another application, the name of the application menu will change to that app, & the menus in the menu bar will also change.

Active app Active app window

Finder

Finder on your device

The Finder, represented by a blue smiley face icon , is where you can organize & gain access to almost everything on your MacBook Air, including videos, pictures, documents, and other files. Click on the Finder icon in the Dock at the lower part of your display to open a Finder window.

Finder

Stay organized. Your device has folders designed for basic content—Music, Apps, Documents, Downloads, etc. As you create documents, download applications, and perform other tasks, you can create new folders to ensure your files are kept in the right place. To create a new folder, click on the **File** button in the menu bar, and then click on the **New Folder** button in the menu that pops-up.

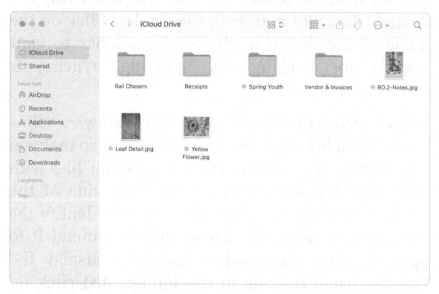

The Finder window: To change how folders & documents are shown in Finder, click on the pop-up menu icon in the top of the Finder window. You can view your files in a gallery⬚, in hierarchical columns⬚, in list view⬚, or as icons⬚. The side bar on the left side of the Finder window displays the things you use regularly or the things you want to open quickly. To view all the files saved in iCloud Drive, click on the **iCloud Drive** folder on the side bar. To change what is displayed on the sidebar, simply click on the **Finder** button in the menu bar, click on the **Settings** button in the menu that pops-up, and then make the necessary changes.

Synchronize devices: After connecting a device like an iPad or iPhone to your MacBook Air, the device's data will appear in the Finder, Click on the name of the device in the Finder sidebar to view options for backing up, updating, syncing & restoring your device.

Gallery view: Gallery View and Column view allow you to see a big overview of selected files so that you can identify your videos, pictures, & other files with ease. The Preview Panel on the right side of the window displays info that can help you identify the file you're looking for. Press Shift-Command-P to open or close the preview panel. To display the Preview panel options in the Finder, just click on **View** in the menu bar, and then click on **Show Preview** in the menu that pops-up. To customize what is displayed, click on **View** in the menu bar, click on **Show Preview Options** in the menu that appears, and then select options for the type of file.

Tip: To show file names in Gallery view, press Command-J & choose Show file name.

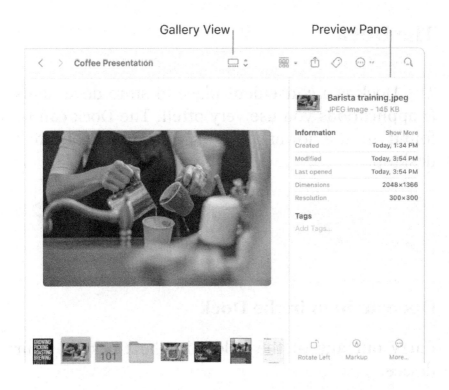

You can click on the More Options icon⊙ in the lower right corner of the window to see shortcuts that can be used to manage & edit files in the Finder.

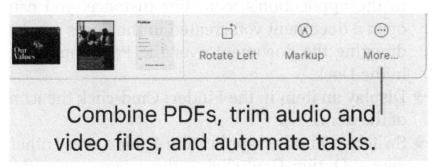

Combine PDFs, trim audio and video files, and automate tasks.

The Dock

The Dock is a convenient place to store documents & applications you use very often. The Dock can be found in the lower part of your MacBook Air's desktop.

Open an item in the Dock

Carry out any of the below in the Dock on your device:

→ Launch an application: Click on the application's icon. For instance, click on the FaceTime app icon to open the FaceTime application.
→ Open a file in an application by dragging the file to the application's icon. For instance, you can open a document you created in the Pages app by dragging the document over the Pages app icon in the Dock.
→ Display an item in the Finder: Cmd-click the icon of the item.
→ Switch to another application & hide every other app: Option-Cmd-click the icon of the application you want to use.

➔ Go to the previous application & hide the application you are currently using: Option-click the icon of the application you are currently using.

Close an application: Click on the red dot in the upper left part of an open window to close the window (the application will remain open). Open applications have black dots under them on the Dock. To close an application, ctrl-click the application's icon in the Dock and then click on **Quit** when it appears.

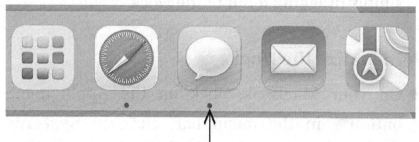

Open apps have a black dot beneath them in the Dock

Remove or add Dock items

Carry out any of the below on your MacBook Air:

→ Add an app, file, or folder to the Dock: You can add an application to the Dock by simply dragging the application to the left side of the Dock. Drag folders & files to the right side of the Dock on your device.

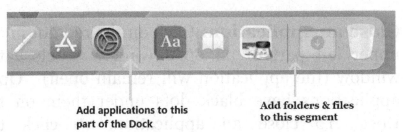

Add applications to this part of the Dock

Add folders & files to this segment

→ Remove applications, files, or folders from the Dock: You can remove an item from the Dock by simply dragging it out of the Dock.

Personalize the Dock

→ On your MacBook, click on the Apple menu button in the menu bar, click on **Systems Settings** in the menu that appears, and then click on Desktop & Dock in the side bar of the window that opens(you might have to scroll down).

→ Under Dock on the right side of the window, make changes to any of the options.
For example, you can change the size of the icons in the Dock, the location of the Dock, or even hide the Dock.

Click on the Help button ? in the lower part of the window to get more information about the options.

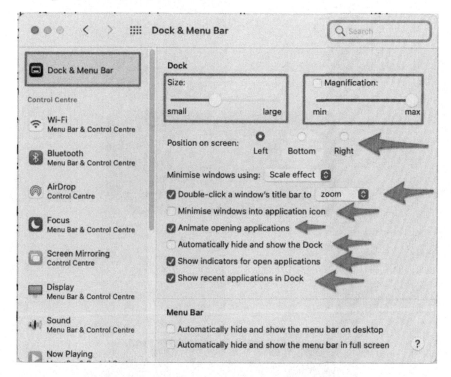

Notifications Center

The Notifications Center keeps all your important info in one place on your MacBook Air. In the Notifications Centre, you can find the notifications you've missed, and get details about the weather, stocks, and more; you can also customize widgets.

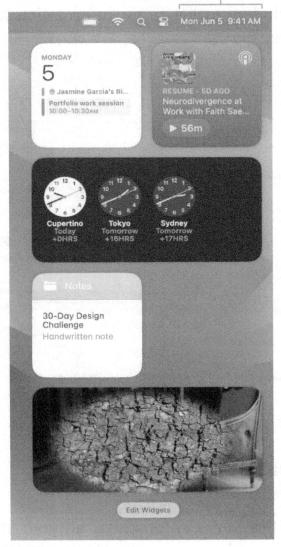

Click to open
Notification Center.

Open or close the Notifications Center

48

→ To enter the Notifications Centre, just click on the time & date in the upper left corner of the screen, or use 2 fingers to swipe to the left from the right edge of your MacBook Air's trackpad.

→ To exit & close the Notifications Centre, simply click anywhere on your desktop or click on the time & date in the upper left corner of your display.

Focus: Activate a Focus mode to reduce distractions when you want to concentrate on a certain task. Focus can block all notifications or allow only some to appear, and it can use statuses in the Messages application to let your contacts know that your notifications have been silenced. To configure the Focus feature, click the Apple menu button in the upper left corner of your screen, click on **Systems Settings** in the menu that pops-up, and then click on the **Focus** button in the sidebar.

You can personalize the Focus feature to suit what you are doing at the moment and only receive notifications from certain individuals or applications.

Add a Focus filter.

Schedule a Focus.

To activate or deactivate the Focus feature, click on the Controls Center icon in the upper right corner of your display, then click on the Focus segment & pick one of the Focus modes.

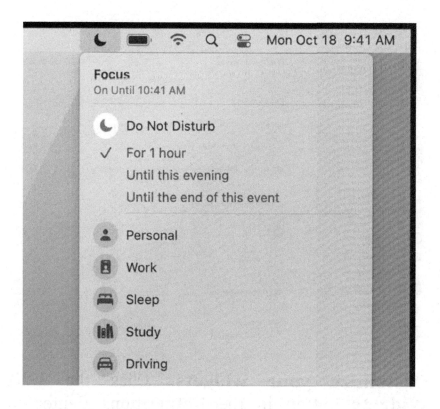

Interact with your alerts: Respond to e-mails, listen to podcasts, or check calendar event info. Click on the arrow in the upper right edge of a notification to see options, take actions, or get more details.

Configure notification settings: Click on the Apple menu button in the upper left corner of your display, click on **Systems Settings** in the menu that pops-up, click on the **Notifications** button, and then choose which notifications you'd like to see.

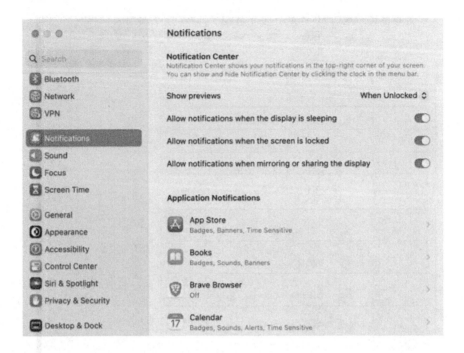

Customize your widgets: Click the **Edit Widgets** button in the Notifications Center to remove, add, or re-organize widgets.

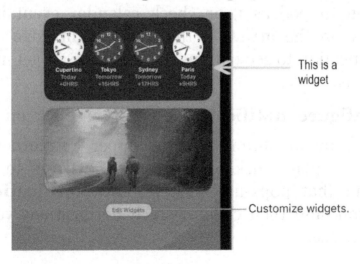

This is a widget

Customize widgets.

Control Center

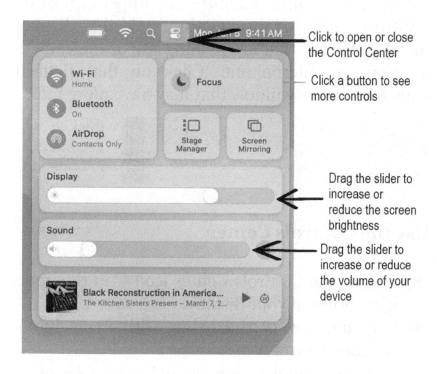

Click to open or close the Control Center

Click a button to see more controls

Drag the slider to increase or reduce the screen brightness

Drag the slider to increase or reduce the volume of your device

The Controls Center provides fast access to important macOS settings like Bluetooth, Stage Manager, and more. You can personalize the Controls Centre and add more features.

When you see an orange dot beside the Control Centre icon in the menu bar, it means your

MacBook Air's microphone is in use; a green dot means your mac's camera is being used, and an arrow ◢ means your location is being used. When you open the Controls Centre, the upper part of the Controls Centre might contain a field that displays the applications that are making use of the camera, location, or microphone. Click on that field to launch a Privacy window that may have more info.

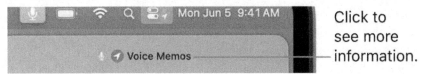

Click to
see more
—— information.

Use the Controls Center

➜ Click on the Controls Center icon in the upper right corner of your display.
➜ Carry out any of the below with items in the Controls Centre:

- Move a slider to reduce or increase a setting, for instance, you can drag the Display slider to change your Mac's screen brightness.
- Click on an icon to activate or deactivate a feature, for instance, click WiFi or AirDrop to activate or deactivate it
- Click an item or the item's arrow to display more options— for instance, click on the **Focus** button to display your Focus list and enable or deactivate a Focus mode.

54

Personalize the Controls Center

➔ Click the Apple menu button ⬛ in the upper left edge of your display, click on **Systems Settings** in the menu that pops-up, and then click on Control Centre on the sidebar.

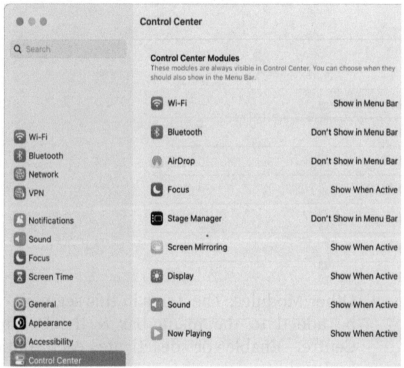

➔ Select the settings for the items in these segments on the right side of the window.

- Controls Centre Modules: The components of this segment are always displayed in the Controls Centre; you cannot remove these items from the Control Centre. You can choose to add these items to the items in the menu bar. Click on the drop-down menu beside an item, and then pick one of the options.

- Menu bar only: You can add more items to the menu bar.

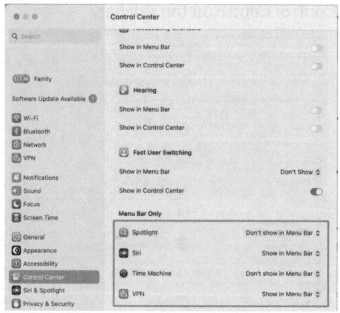

- Other Modules: The items in this segment can be added to the menu bar & the Controls Centre. Enable or deactivate each option under an item.

Launchpad

Launchpad is a central location on your MacBook Air where you can browse & launch applications.

After installing an application from the App Store, it will appear in Launchpad.

Open & close Launchpad

➔ Click on the Launchpad icon ⦙⦙⦙ in the Dock to open Launchpad on your device.

➔ Press the **Esc** key on your keyboard to close Launchpad without launching an application.

Find & launch applications in Launchpad

➔ Find an application: Enter the application's name in the search bar in the upper part of Launchpad. Or, check the next page in Launchpad—Press

Cmd-Right Arrow or Command-Left Arrow, or use a finger to swipe right or left on your mac's trackpad.
→ Click an app's icon to open it

Organize applications in Launchpad

→ You can move an application around a page by dragging it to another location on that page.
→ You can move an application to another page by dragging the application to the edge of your MacBook's screen, and then releasing the application when you enter the next page.
→ You can create an app folder by dragging an application over another application.
→ Change a folder's name: Click on the folder to open it, click on the folder's name, and then insert another name.
→ To add more applications to the folder, simply drag the applications over the folder.
→ You can remove an application from a folder by dragging it out of the folder.

Remove applications from Launchpad

→ Open Launchpad, and then long-press the Option button on the keyboard or long-click an application till all the applications start jiggling.

➔ Click the application's Remove icon⊗, and then click on the **Delete** button in the menu that appears.

System Settings

You can personalize all your MacBook's settings in Systems Setting. For instance, you can activate and personalize the Hover Text feature in System Settings. You can also download new software updates.

Personalize your device.

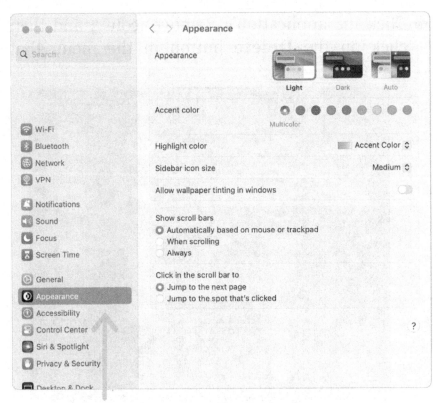

Click one of the items in the sidebar to make adjustments to it settings

Click on the Systems Settings icon in the Dock or click on the Apple menu button in the upper left corner of your display, click on **Systems Setting** in the menu that pops-up, and then click on any of the settings in the sidebar that you'd like to personalize. You may need to scroll down to see additional settings.

Find options in the System Settings

Search box   Options that match what you searched

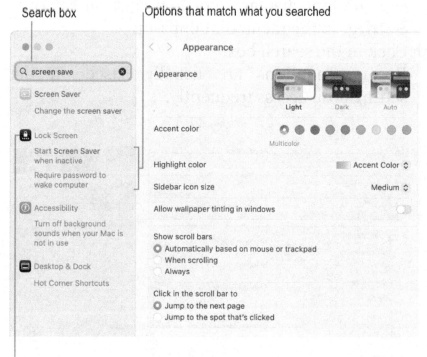

A setting with options that match what you searched

If you don't know where a certain setting is in **Systems Setting**, use the search box in the upper left part of the window. Settings with options that match what you entered in the search box will be displayed below.

Choose one of the suggested settings

➡ Click the Apple menu icon in the upper left edge of your display, and then click on **System Setting** in the menu that pops-up

➡ Click in the search box.

Recommendations are usually based on the settings you access frequently.

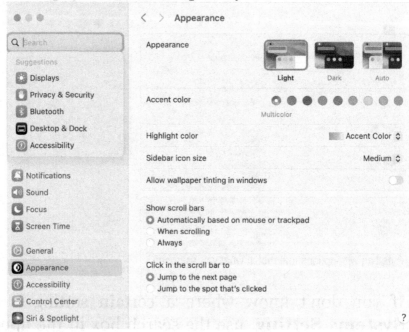

➡ Click on one of the available suggestions

Update macOS: Click the Apple menu icon in the upper left edge of your display, click on **System Setting** in the menu that pops-up, click the **General** button, and then click Software Updates to see if your MacBook Air is using the latest version of macOS software. You can set the automatic software update option.

Spotlight

The Spotlight feature allows MacBook Air users to easily find anything on their device (like contacts, files, pictures, e-mails, etc.).

Type what you want in the search field

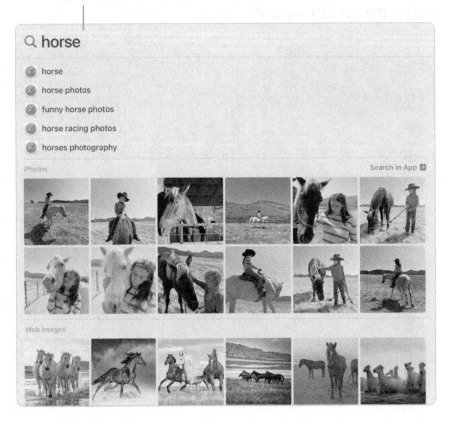

Find something

➔ Carry out any of the below on your MacBook Air:

> Click on the Spotlight icon 🔍 in the upper right corner of the screen.

> Press Command-Space bar to show or hide the Spotlight search box.

- ➤ Press the Spotlight button  on your keyboard.
- → Type what you want in the search bar.
- → Click on any of the results in the search results.
- → To view all the results from your MacBook Air in the Finder, scroll to the end of the results list, and then click the **Search in Finder** button.

Get conversions & calculations in Spotlight

< 25 lbs

25 pounds
11.34 kilograms

0.012	short tons
400	ounces
11,339.81	grams
11,339,809.25	milligrams

You can type mathematical expressions, currency rates, temperatures, or measurements in the Spotlight search bar and get conversions or calculations.

→ For Calculations: Enter a mathematical expression like 386 * 27.90 or 1472/73.

→ To convert currency: Enter an amount for instance $537, 9443 krone, or "3932 yen in euros".

→ Temperature Conversion: Enter a temperature for example 473.2F, 94C, or 402K in F.

→ Measurement Conversion: Enter measurements for example 92lbs, 74yards, 65stone, or "87ft to meters".

→ World clock conversion: Type a short sentence about the time in a place, like "Dubai local time" or "time in China."

Apple ID

Your Apple ID is an account that allows you to gain access to all Apple services. When you have an Apple ID, you can download applications from the Applications Store; gain access to media in Apple TV, Apple Podcasts, Apple Music, & Apple Books; Update content on all your devices using iCloud; setup a family sharing group; etc.

Note: If you forget your Apple ID login code, you do not have to setup another Apple ID. Simply, click on "Forget Apple ID or Password"? link in the login window to retrieve your passcode.

All in one place: Control everything related to your Apple ID in System Settings. Enter Systems Setting —you'll find your Apple ID & Family Sharing settings in the upper part of the side bar. Click on the **Sign in with your Apple ID** button to log in with your Apple ID if you haven't done that before.

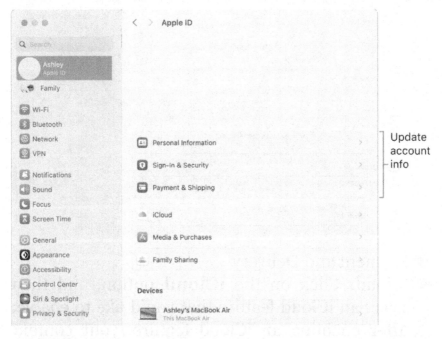

Update your security, account, & payment info. In Systems Setting, click on your Apple ID at the top of the sidebar, then choose one of the items to review & update your account details.

→ Overview: The Overview segment allows you to know if your account is setup & working properly.

→ Personal Info

→ Sign-In & Security

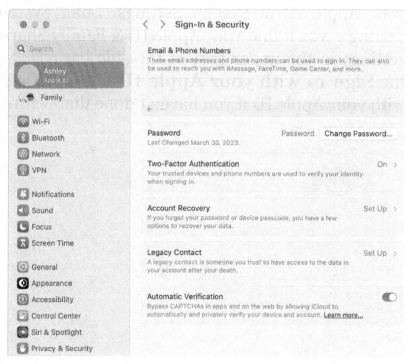

→ Payment and Delivery

→ ICloud: Click on the **iCloud** option, and then select an iCloud feature that you'd like to enable. After enabling an iCloud feature, your content will be stored in iCloud, not on your MacBook Air, so you can gain access to the content on any device by simply enabling iCloud on the device & logging in with your Apple ID.

→ Media and purchases: Manage accounts associated with Apple Podcasts, Apple TV, Apple Music, & Apple Books; choose the purchase settings; & manage your membership.

Check all your devices. View the devices that are using your Apple ID. You can check the iCloud backup status for an iPad or iPhone, or remove a device from your account if it's no longer yours.

Family Sharing

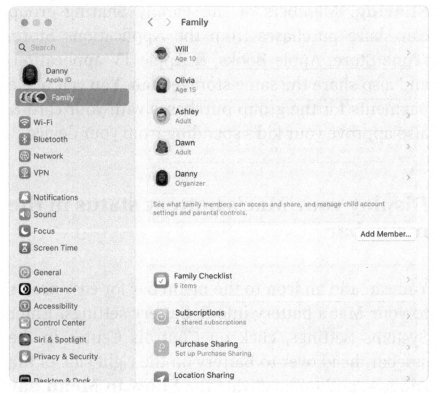

Family Sharing allows you to create a family group (consisting of about 6 members) where you can share & manage purchases, share device locations, etc. You can also control how your kid uses their device by creating an Apple ID account for the child and setting Screen Time limits. To manage Family Sharing settings, click on **Family** in Systems setting, then select the options you want on the right side of the window.

Share storage & purchases with Family Sharing. Members of the Family Sharing group can share purchases from the Applications Store, iTune Store, Apple Books, & Apple TV application, and also share the same storage plan. You can make payments for the group purchases with your card & also approve your kid's spending from your device

Display your Mac's battery status in the menu bar

You can add an icon to the menu bar for easy access to your Mac's battery info & Battery settings. Enter Systems Settings, click on Controls Center in the sidebar, head over to Battery on the right side of the window, and then activate the **Show in Menu bar** option to display your battery's status in the menu bar. You can also activate the **Show Percentage option** to display the battery percentage in the menu bar.

Adjust the battery settings. Set different options for your MacBook's battery.

→ **Optimized battery charging**: This feature allows your MacBook Air to learn your charging routine in order to help reduce wear & tear on your battery and improve the battery's lifespan. This feature delays charging the battery past 80 percent when it predicts that you will charge the battery for an extended period & aims to fully charge the battery before your device is unplugged. In Systems Settings, click on the **Battery** option in the side bar, click on the Information icon ⓘ in the Battery health segment on the right side of the window, and then enable the **Optimized Battery Charging** feature.

→ **Low Power Mode:** Enable this feature to reduce the use of energy & increase your battery life. It's a great choice for long trips or when you are away from a power source. Click on the Apple

Menu button ⚫ in the menu bar, click on **System Settings** in the menu that appears, click on the **Battery** button in the side bar, and then select from the options in the Low Power Mode drop-down menu.

Check the battery charge: Check the status icon on the right end of the menus bar to view the charging status or the current battery level. Or enter Systems Settings and then click on the **Battery** option in the sidebar.

Save battery power. To extend battery life on a single charge, you can decrease your Mac's screen brightness, close applications you are not using, and remove peripheral devices you aren't using.

Battery usage history: Click on the Apple Menu icon ⚫ in the menu bar, click on **System Settings** in the menu that pops up & click on the **Battery** button in the side bar to view your battery usage for the last twenty-four hours or ten days.

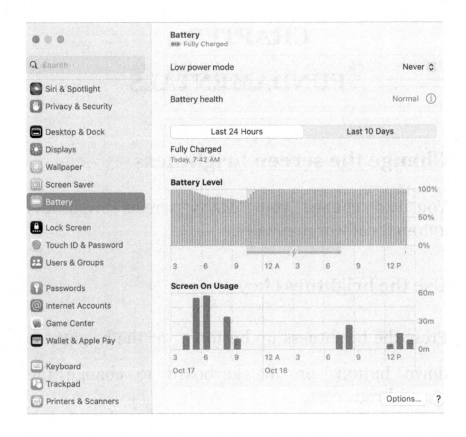

CHAPTER 4

FUNDAMENTALS

Change the screen brightness

You can change your Mac's screen brightness automatically or manually.

Use the brightness key

Press the brightness up button ☀ or the brightness down button ☀ on the keyboard to change the screen brightness.

Automatically change your screen brightness

Your device can use its ambient light sensor to automatically change the screen brightness to match the lighting around you.

→ Click on the Apple menu icon in the upper left corner of your display, click **Systems Setting** in the menu that appears, and then click on the Displays ⚙ button on the sidebar.

➔ Activate the **"Automatically Adjust Brightness"** feature on the right side of the window.

Adjust the brightness manually

➔ Click on the Apple menu icon in the upper left corner of your display, click **Systems Setting** in the menu that appears, and then click on the Displays button on the sidebar.

→ Slide the Brightness slider on the right side of the window to change your mac's screen brightness.

Connect your MacBook Air to the Internet

You can connect to the Internet with your MacBook Air. The 2 most common ways to access the Internet are through Ethernet (wired) or WiFi (wireless) connection.

Use WiFi

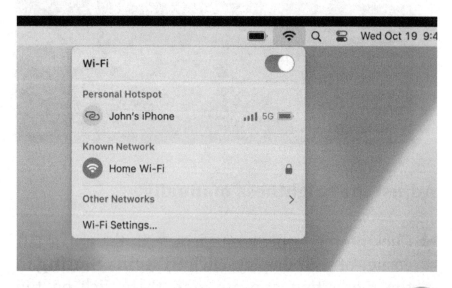

If a WiFi network is available, the WiFi button will be displayed in the upper right corner of your screen. Click on the WiFi button, and then pick one of the networks to join. If there's a lock icon🔒 next to the name of the network, it means the network is passcode-protected - you have to insert the WiFi passcode before you can make use of the WiFi network.

To connect to a hidden WiFi network, simply click on the WiFi button 📶 displayed in the upper right corner of your screen, click on the **Other Networks** button, click on **Other** in the bottom of the Other Network list, type the network's name in the Network Name box, click on the Security drop-down menu and then select the network's security. Enter all important info in the appropriate fields, and then click on the **Join** button.

Using Ethernet

Use an Ethernet either through an Ethernet network or via a cable modem or DSL. Use an adapter to connect the Ethernet cable to the Thunderbolt or USB port on your MacBook Air.

In most cases, your MacBook Air will be connected to the Internet automatically. If not, adhere to the steps below to access network settings. If you aren't sure what to enter, contact your internet service provider or network administrator.

➔ Click the Apple menu icon⬤ in the menu bar, and then click on **Systems Settings** in the menu that pops up.

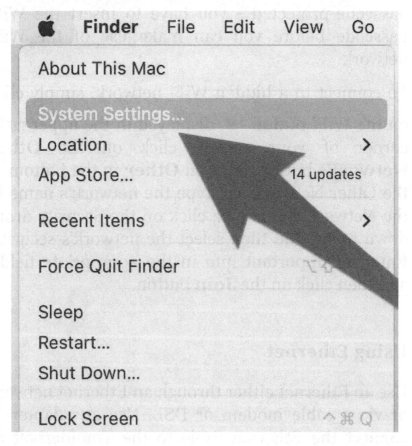

➔ Click on the **Network**⊕ button in the sidebar of the window, click on the Ethernet Service⬤ on the right, and then click on the **Details** button.

→ Enable or disable Limit IP Address Tracking if you wish.

→ Click on TCP / IP on the sidebar, select the Configure IPv4 drop-down menu, and select the configuration method recommended by your internet service provider.

- Use DHCP: Pick this option if your internet service provider did not send a specific IP address to you.

- Use DHCP with manual address: Pick this option if you were sent a specific IP address & your internet service provider uses DHCP, and then insert the IP address.

- Manually: Pick this option if your internet service provider sent a specific IP address, a router address, & a subnet mask to you, and then insert those values.

→ If you were sent WINS settings, click on the WINS button in the side bar and then fill in the info you received.

→ If you were sent DNS server or search domain settings, click on DNS in the side bar and then fill in the info you received.

→ If you received Ethernet hardware settings, click on the **Hardware** button in the sidebar, and then fill in the details you received

→ If you were sent proxy server settings, click on the Proxy button in the side bar and then fill on the info you received.

→ Click the **OK** button.

View & edit files with Quick Look

Rotate the image

Markup | Share the file with others

Open with Preview

The **Quick Look** feature provides a quick, full-size overview of almost any file without opening it. You can rotate images, trim videos & audio, and annotate—in the Quick Look window.

→ On your MacBook Air, select an item (Hover the cursor over the item, and then click on the item to select it) or select many items (Hold down the Command key on your keyboard, and then click the items), and then press the Space bar on your keyboard to open a Quick Look window.

→ Do any of the below in the Quick Look window:

- Change the window's size: Click on the Full-Screen icon⊘ in the upper left edge of the window or drag the window's corners. To leave full-screen, hover the cursor to the lower part of the window, and then click the Restore Down icon ↘↖ that appears.

- Click on the Rotate icon⃞ to rotate the item to the left or long-press the Option button on the keyboard, and then click on the Rotate icon ⃞ to rotate the item to the right. Keep clicking the icon to continue rotating the item.

- Zoom: Press **Cmd-+** to zoom in or the **Cmd-minus** keyboard combination to zoom out of the item.

81

- Click on the Markup icon Ⓐ to markup an item.
- Trim audio or video clips: Click on the Trim icon ▸▢◂ , and then drag the yellow handle in the trim panel. Click on the Play button ▶ to preview the adjustments you have made. Click the **Revert** button to start over. After trimming the file, click on the **Done** button then replace the original file or save it as a new file.
- Share an item: click the Share icon ⬆, and then choose from the available sharing options.
- Check other items (if you have selected more than one item): Click on the arrows in the upper left corner of the window, or simply press the Right Arrow button or the Left Arrow button on your keyboard. If the Quick Look window is in full screen, you can click on the Play icon to see the items as a slideshow.
- Display items in Grid view (if you selected more than one item): Click the Grid View icon ▦ or press the Command-Return keyboard combination.
- Copy the item's subject: If the item is a picture, you can isolate the picture's subject from the background. Ctrl-click the picture,

and then click on the **Copy Subject** button. You can paste the subject in a note, e-mail, or document.

→ When you are finished, press the Space bar or click on the Close icon 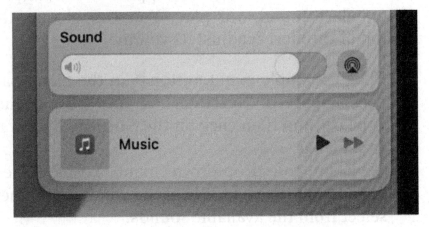 to close the window.

When you a Live Picture in the Quick Look window, the video part of the picture will play automatically. Click on the **Live Photo** button in the lower-left corner of the image to view it again.

Increase or reduce your Mac's volume

→ Click on the Sound controls icon in the Controls Center or menu bar, and then drag the Sound slider to the right or left to change your mac's volume level.

If you can't find the Sounds control icon in the menu bar, you can add it, to do this; simply click the Apple menu button ⍟ in the menu bar, click on **Systems Settings** in the menu that pops up, and then click on the **Controls Center** button in the sidebar on the left side of the window. Click on the drop-down menu beside Sound on the right side of the window, and then select an option.

→ Use the volume buttons in the FN keys row on your MacBook Air's keyboard.

Change your Mac's alert sounds

When you're about to do something that's not allowed, or your MacBook Air needs input or more details, an alert message will appear on the display & an alert sound will play. You can change the sound of the alert & adjust its volume.

→ Click the Apple menu button ⍟ in the menu bar, click **System Settings** in the menu that appears, and then click on the **Sounds** button in the sidebar.

→ Click on the drop-down menu beside "Alert sounds" on the right side of the window and then select from the available sounds.

84

An alert tone will play when it's selected.

→ Do any of the below to change the alert sound:

- Change alert volume level: Move the Alert volume slider. The alert volume is dependent on your MacBook's volume, so if you reduce your MacBook's volume, the alert sounds will be quieter.

- Hear user interface sound effects: Your device will play sound effects when you carry out certain actions, like when you drag something to the trash. To disable these sound effects, disable the "Play users interface sounds effect" setting.

- If you'd like to hear a startup sound when you restart your MacBook Air, simply enable the **Play sound on startup** feature.

- Hear sound effects when you change your MacBook's volume: On some keyboards, when you press a volume button, a sound is played so you can hear the new volume level. To stop this sound from playing, deactivate the "**Play feedback when volume is changed**" feature.

You can also configure your device to flash the screen when it receives an alert. To do this, simply click the Apple menu icon in the menu bar, click on the **System Settings** button in the menu pops-up, and then click on the **Accessibility** button in the sidebar. Click the **Audio** button on the right side of the window, and then enable the **"Flash the screen when alerts sound occurs"** feature.

Take a screenshot or record your MacBook's screen

You can snap or record your MacBook Air's display using the Screenshots feature or keyboard shortcuts. **Screenshot** provides a toolbar that allows you to snap or record the screen easily, with options to control what you're capturing.

Use the Screenshot feature

→ Press Shift-Cmd-5 to launch the Screenshot feature & show the toolbar.
You can also launch Screenshots from Launchpad.

→ Click on any of the tools in the toolbar to highlight what you want to record or snap.
To capture a part of your MacBook's screen, simply drag the frame to change its position or

drag the edges to change the size of the area you'd like to record or snap.

- Click the Record Full-Screen icon to record the whole display.

- Click on the Window icon to snap a window

- Click the Record Section icon to record a part of your MacBook's display.

- Click the Full-Screen icon to snap the whole display.

- Click on the Section icon to snap a part of your MacBook's display.

→ If you want, click on Options.
The "Show Floating Thumbnail" option makes it easier to work with a finished screen recording or screenshot—it floats in the lower right corner of your screen for some seconds, so you have time to drag the file into documents, draw or write in the file, or share the file before saving it.

→ Start recording your screen or taking screenshots:

- For the full display or a section of it: Click on the **Capture** button.

- For a window: Hover your cursor to the window, and then click on the window.
- For recording: Click the **Record** button. To stop recording, click on the Stop Recording icon⊙ in the upper part of your screen.

With Show Floating Thumbnail, you can carry out any of the below while the thumbnail is displayed in the lower right corner of your display:

- Drag the thumbnail into an e-mail, Finder window, note, etc.
- Swipe to the right to store the file on your device.
- Click on the thumbnail to open a window where you can write or draw in the picture, cut the video clip, or share the file with others.

Use keyboard shortcuts to capture photos of your screen

- To take a picture of the whole screen, press the Shift-Cmd-3 keyboard combination.
- To snap part of your screen, press the Shift-Command-4 keyboard combination, and then hover the pointer to the part of your display you want to capture. Press the trackpad or mouse button, drag over the section of your

display you'd like to capture, and then release the trackpad or mouse button.

- To snap the menu bar or a window, press the Shift-Command-4 keyboard combination, and then press the Space bar. Hover the cursor over the menu bar or window to select it, and then click.

- To launch the Screenshot application and display the toolbar, press the Shift-Command 5 keyboard combination.

To personalize these keyboard shortcuts, click the Apple menu icon in the menu bar, click the Systems Settings button in the menu, click the Keyboards button on the sidebar, click on Keyboard Shortcuts on the right side of the window, and then click Screenshots (if necessary, scroll down).

Screen Recordings are stored in MOV format, while Screenshots are saved in PNG format.

Use Touch ID

You can use Touch ID to unlock your device, authenticate purchases, log into 3rd-party applications, and more.

Touch ID & Password

Password

A login password has been set for this user   Change...

Touch ID
Touch ID lets you use your fingerprint to unlock your Mac and make purchases with
Apple Pay, iTunes Store, App Store, and Apple Books.

Finger 1   Add Fingerprint

Use Touch ID to unlock your Mac

Use Touch ID for Apple Pay

Use Touch ID for purchases in iTunes Store, App Store,
and Apple Books

Use Touch ID for autofilling passwords

Use Touch ID for fast user switching

?

Configure Touch ID

➔ Click the Apple menu icon in the menu bar, click the **Systems Settings** button, and click on the **Touch ID & Password** button on the left side of the window.

➔ Click the **Add Fingerprint** button

Touch ID
Touch ID lets you use your fingerprint to unlock your Mac and make purchases with
Apple Pay, iTunes Store, App Store, and Apple Books.

Finger 1   Add Fingerprint

Use Touch ID to unlock your Mac

➔ Insert your passcode, and then adhere to the directives on your screen.
You can find the Touch ID sensor after the FN keys in the upper right part of the keyboard. You can add up to 3 fingerprints to your user account.

➔ Choose how you want to use the Touch ID feature:

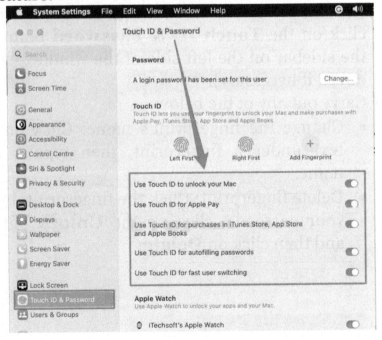

- Unlock your MacBook Air
- Apps Store, iTunes Store, & Apple Books.
- Quick user switching: Use Touch ID to switch from one user account to another.
- Authenticate Apple Pay
- Password AutoFill: Use Touch ID to automatically fill in usernames & passcodes, and automatically fill in credit card information when prompted while making use of Safari & other applications.

Delete or change the name of fingerprints

➔ Click the Apple menu icon in the menu bar, click on the **Systems Settings** button, and then click on the **Touch ID & Password** button in the sidebar on the left side of the window (scroll down, if necessary).

➔ Carry out any of the below:
  - Change the fingerprint's name: Click on the text under a fingerprint, then type a new name.
  - Delete fingerprint: Click the fingerprint, insert your passcode, click on the **Unlock** button, and then click on **Delete**.

Use Touch ID to unlock, sign in, or change users on your MacBook Air

→ Unlock your MacBook & some passcode-protected items: After waking your MacBook Air from sleep or opening any passcode-protected item, just put your registered finger on the Touch ID sensor in the upper right corner of the keyboard when **told** to.

→ Sign in from the sign-in window: Click your name in the sign-in window, then put your registered finger on the Touch ID sensor in the upper right corner of the keyboard.

Increase the size of everything on your screen

You can change the resolution of your display to make everything on your screen appear bigger.

→ Click the Apple menu icon in the menu bar, click the **System Setting** button, and then click Display in the side bar.

→ Choose any of the resolutions on the right side of the window.

A lower resolution makes everything on the screen larger.

Change text size

→ In applications: You can press Cmd-Plus (+) or Cmd-Minus (-) to change the text size.

→ In desktop labels: Ctrl-click on the desktop, click Show View Option, click on the Text Size menu, and then choose one of the options.

→ In webpages: Visit a website in the Safari application, and then press Command-Option-Plus (+) to increase the text size or press Command-Option-Minus (-) to reduce it

→ In sidebars: Click the Apple menu icon in the menu bar, click on Systems Settings, and then click on the **Appearance** button in the sidebar on the left side of the window. Click on the drop-down menu close to "sidebar icon size" on the right side of the window, and then select **Large**.

→ In folder & file names in the Finder: Click on View, click on Show View Option. Click on the Text Size drop-down menu, and then select one of the options.

Change icons size

→ On the desktop: Ctrl-click on the desktop, click Show View Option, and then move the Icon Size slider by dragging it to the left or right.

→ In sidebars: Click the Apple Menu icon🍎 in the menu bar, click **Systems Settings**, and then click the **Appearance** button in the sidebar on the left side of the window. Click the drop-down menu close to "Sidebar icon size" on the right side of the window, and then select one of the options.

→ In the Finder window: Click on View, click on Show View Option. In List view & Icon view, pick any of the icon sizes. You can pick a bigger thumbnail size in the Gallery view.

Use Hover Text

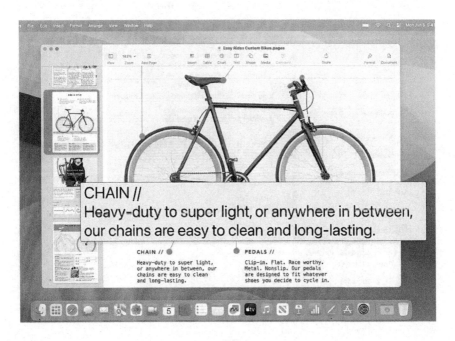

The Hover Text feature allows your device to show a zoomed version of any text you highlight with your mouse.

Enable and customize Hover Text

→ Click the Apple menu icon in the menu bar, click the **System Setting** button in the menu, click on Accessibility in the sidebar on the left side of the window, and then click on **Zoom** on the right side of the window.
→ Activate the **Hover Text** feature

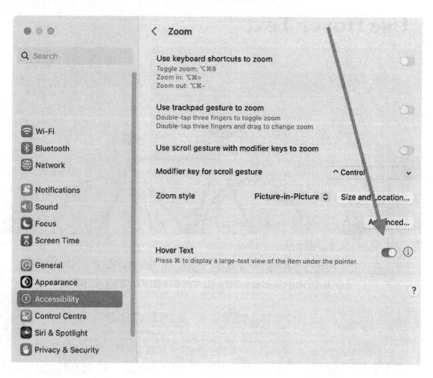

To personalize the Hover Text feature, click the Information icon ⓘ beside Hover Text, and then customize any of the below:

- The window's position when you enter text. Click on the "Texts-entry location" drop-down menu and choose any of the options. If you do not want the window to appear while you type, simply select the **None** option.
  While typing, a large version of what you are typing will appear in a window in the location you picked.
- The modifier button you press to activate the Hover Text feature. Click the "Activation Modifier" drop-down menu and pick one of the options. By default, you can enable the Hover Text feature by pressing the Command button.

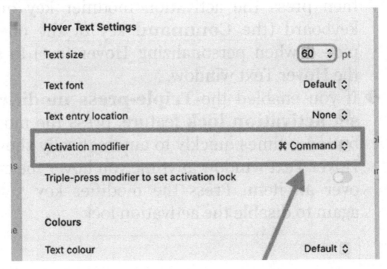

97

You can set Hover Text to automatically appear when you hover the cursor over an item, without having to press a button on the keyboard every time. To do this, simply enable **Triple-press modifier to set activation lock**, then when you want the Hover Text feature to be active for a certain period — like when you are filling a form — triple-press the selected modifier key. Triple-press the modifier key again to deactivate the activation lock

- The text size, font, and colours used in the window.

Use Hover Text

→ Move the cursor over an item on your screen, and then press the activation modifier key on the keyboard (the **Command** key or the one you picked when personalizing Hover text) to show the Hover Text window.

→ If you enabled the **Triple-press modifier to set activation lock** feature, press the modifier button 3 times quickly to automatically show the Hover Text window anytime you hover the cursor over an item. Press the modifier key 3 times again to disable the activation lock

Change the size & colour of the pointer

➜ Click on the Apple menu icon in the menu bar, click on the **System Setting** button, click Accessibility in the sidebar on the left side of the window, and then click on **Display** on the right side of the window.

➜ Head over to Pointer and then set any of the below:

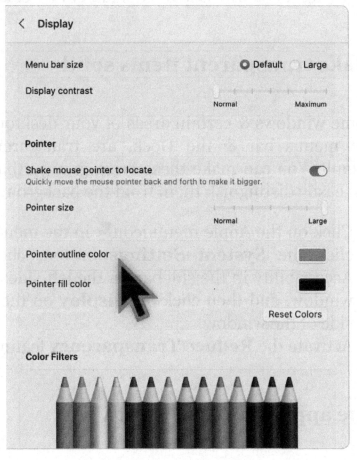

- Shake the mouse pointer to locate: Activate this feature to make the cursor bigger anytime you quickly move your finger on the trackpad or when you move the mouse around quickly.
- Pointer size: Drag the slider to the right or left to increase or decrease the cursor's size.
- Pointer fill colour
- Pointer outline colour
- Reset colours: Use the default cursor colours

Make transparent items solid

Some windows & certain areas of your desktop, like the menus bar & the Dock, are transparent by default. You can make these areas gray so that you can easily distinguish them from the background.

→ Click on the Apple menu icon in the menu bar, click the **System Settings** button, click on Accessibility in the sidebar on the left side of the window, and then click on **Display** on the right side of the window.
→ Activate the **Reduce Transparency** feature.

Use applications in Split View

The Split View feature allows you to use two applications side by side.

→ While using an app, move the cursor over the green icon in the upper left edge of the app's window, and then click on **Tile Window to the Right side of the Screen** or **Tile the Window to the Left Side of the Screen** from the menu that pops-up

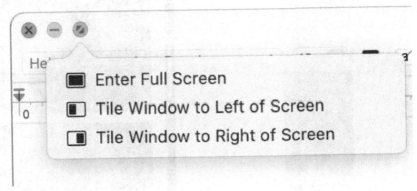

➜ On the other side of your display, click on the other application you'd like to use.

➜ Carry out any of the below in Split View:

- Hide or display the Dock: Hove the cursor to or away from the location of the Dock.

- Hide or display the menu bar: Hover the cursor away from or to the upper edge of your MacBook's screen.

- Hide or display the tools panel & title of a window: Click on the window, then hover the cursor to or away from the upper edge of your MacBook's screen.

- Increase the size of one of the windows: Hover the cursor over the center dividing bar, and then drag it to the right or left side of your display. Click the dividing bar twice quickly to go back to the original size.

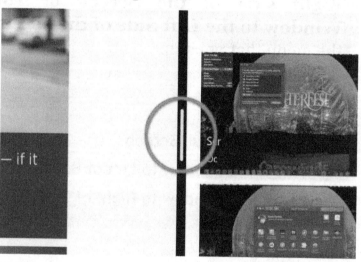

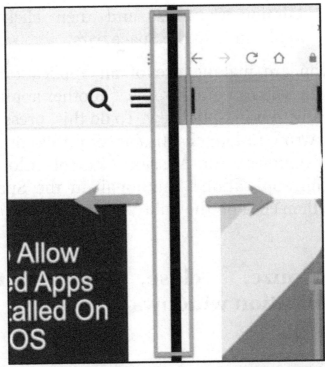

- Use another application on one side: Click on the app's window, hover the cursor over the green icon in the upper left edge of the window, click on the **Replace Tiled Window** button, and then click on the window you'd like to use.
- Show one of the windows in full-screen: Click on the app's window, hover the cursor over the green icon in the upper left edge, and then click the **Make Window Full-Screen** button.

The view the second application in full screen, simply press Control-Up Arrow to open

Mission Controls, and then click on the application in the Space bars.

If you are making use of an application in full-screen, you can quickly select another application to work with it in Split View. To do this, press Control-Up Arrow to launch Mission Controls, drag one of the windows from Mission Control onto the full-screen application's thumbnail in the Space bars, and then click on the Split View thumbnail.

Maximize, close, or minimize application windows

● ● ●   Screen Saver

→ Maximize a window: Long-press the Option button on the keyboard while clicking on the green icon ⊕ in the upper left edge of a window. To go back to the window's previous size, simply Option-click the green icon ⊕ one more time.

→ To close a window, just click the Close icon ✕ in the window or press the Cmd-W keyboard combination. Press Option-Cmd-W to close all windows for an application.

Or, double-click the application's title bar to maximize the window

→ Minimize the window: Click the Yellow Minimize icon ⬤ in the window, or press the Cmd-M keyboard combination.

You can also manually adjust the size of a window by dragging the edge of the window (side, bottom, or top).

Personalize the desktop image

You can change your desktop's wallpaper. Pick from the available colours or images, or use one of your personal photos.

→ Click the Apple menu icon in the menu bar, click the **Systems Settings** button, and then click the **Wallpapers** button in the sidebar on the left side of the window.
→ Pick any of the wallpapers from the available categories:
  • Add Photos/Add Folders or Albums: You can add your personal photos from here.
  • Dynamic Wallpapers: These pictures darken & lighten based on the time of the day.

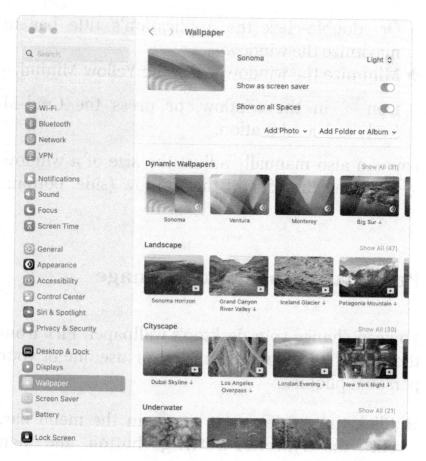

- Shuffle Aerials: These pictures change at scheduled times.
- Landscapes, Earth, Underwater, & Cityscapes.
- Pictures.
- Colours

➔ Set options for your wallpaper.

The options vary depending on the wallpaper you select. For instance, you can carry out any of the below:

- Add your colour
- Select dark or light still version of the wallpapers
- Enable a slow-motion aerial as your MacBook's Screensaver

To quickly use one of the pictures in the Photos application, head over to the Photos application,

select the picture, click on the Share icon ⬆ on the tools panel, and then click the **Set Wallpaper** option.

To use an image you find on the internet as your wallpaper, simply Ctrl-click the picture in the browser and then click on the **Use Image as Desktop Picture** button.

Uninstall applications

You can delete applications that you installed on your MacBook.

➡ Click on the Finder icon 🙂 in the Dock to open Finder, and then click on the **Applications** button in the sidebar on the left side of the window.

➡ Carry out any of the below:

- If the application is in a folder: Open the application's folder to see if it has an Uninstaller. If you see Uninstall [Apps] or [Apps] Uninstaller, click on it twice, and then adhere to the guidelines on your screen.
- If the application is not in a folder or does not have an Uninstaller, just drag the app from the Apps folder to the Trash.

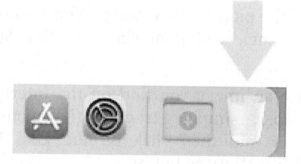

Change your user login photo

You can change the image that's displayed close to your user name in the login window on your device. Your user login photo is also used as your Apple ID photo.

You can use one of your photos, an emoji, Memoji, or monogram, or even snap a new picture with your laptop's Camera.

Click to change the user picture.

➔ Click the Apple menu icon in the menu bar, click the **Systems Setting** button in the menu, and then click on **Users & Group** in the sidebar on the left side of the window.

➔ Click on the user photo close to your login name on the right side of the window, and then perform any of the below:

- Use an emoji: Choose the **Emoji** option, and then click on the Add Emoji icon  to pick a picture from the emoji library. Or pick any of the available emoji and styles.

- Use a Memoji: Choose the **Memoji** option, and then click on the Add icon to pick & compose one for yourself. Or pick any of the available Memoji, then choose a style & pose.

- Snap a picture with your laptop's camera: Choose the **Camera** option. Get ready for the shot, and then click the Capture button.

You can snap the picture as many times as needed.

- Use a monogram: Choose the **Monogram** option, choose one of the background colours, and then type your initials.

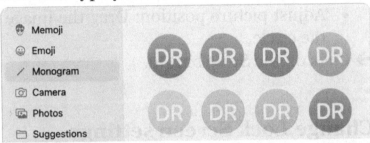

- Use one of the pictures in your Photos library: Choose the **Photos** option. To view pictures from a specific album, click the album, and then choose any of the photos.

- Choose one of the recommended pictures: Choose the **Suggestions** option on the left side of the window, and then pick any of the pictures.

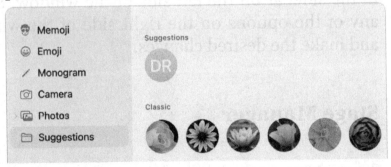

➜ After selecting a picture, you can make adjustments to its appearance. Carry out any of the below:
  - Drag the slider to the right or left to zoom in or out.
  - Adjust picture position: Drag the image inside the circle.
➜ Click on the **Save** button.

Change Lock Screen settings

Use the Lock Screen settings to protect your device from tampering & malware.

To change these settings, click the Apple menu icon in the menu bar, click the **Systems Setting** button, and then click the **Lock Screen** button in the sidebar on the left side of the window. Select any of the options on the right side of the window and make the desired changes.

Stage Manager

Stage Manager places the application you are working on in the middle of your display, and neatly arranges recently used applications on the left corner of your display for fast & easy access.

With the **Stage Manager** feature activated, you can easily move between tasks while keeping the focus on what's in the middle of your display. You can arrange, overlap, & change the size of windows to the layout that you want. You can also arrange multiple applications on your display to work together as a group. When you switch to the group, all the applications in that group will open in the middle of your screen.

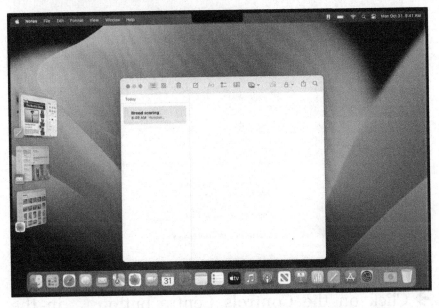

Activate or disable Stage Manager

Carry out any of the below:

➔ Click on the Apple menu icon🍎 in the menu bar, click the **Systems Setting** button in the menu, and then click on Desktop & Dock◼ in the sidebar on the left side of the window. Head over to Desktop & Stage Manager on the right side of the window, then activate or disable Stage Manager

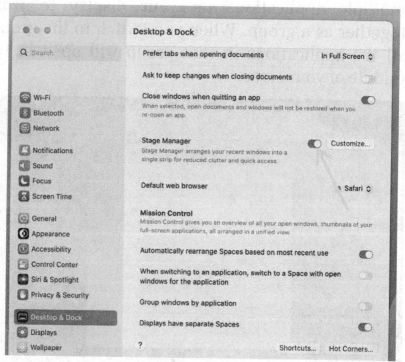

➔ Click on the Controls Centre button⬛ in the upper right corner of your display, and then click the Stage Manager⬛ button to enable or deactivate the **Stage Manager** feature.

Use Stage Manager

Carry out any of the below on your laptop:

→ Switch applications: Click any of the apps on the left side of your MacBook's display.

→ Arrange Windows: Overlap, and change the position & size of the windows to fit your workflow.

➔ Group applications: Drag an application from the left corner of your MacBook's display to add it to a group of applications in the middle of your display.

➔ Ungroup applications: Drag an application from the middle of your display to the left side.

If you disable "**Show recent applications in Stage Manager**" in Stage Manager settings, the applications list on the left side of your screen will be hidden. Hover the cursor to the left edge of your display to reveal the list.

Display or hide Stage Manager in the menu bar

You can add the Stage Manager button to the menu bar.

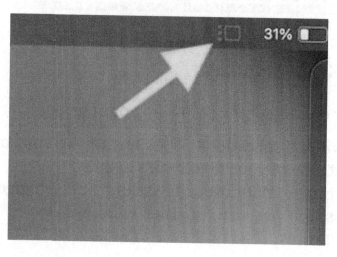

➡ Click the Apple menu icon in the menu bar, click the **Systems Setting** button in the menu, and then click on the **Controls Center** button in the sidebar on the left side of the window.

➡ Click on the drop-down menu close to the Stage Manager feature on the right side of the window, and then pick one of the options.

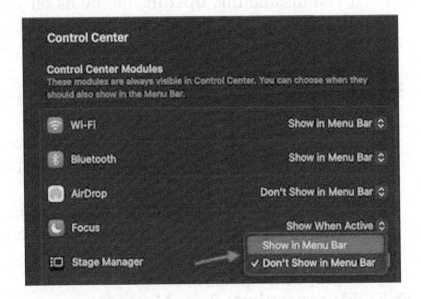

Change Stage Manager settings

➡ Click the Apple Menu icon in the menu bar on your MacBook, click the **Systems Setting** button in the menu that appears, and then click on Desktop & Dock in the sidebar on the left side of the window.

117

→ Head over to Desktop & Stage Manager on the right side of the window

→ Select or unselect the checkboxes beside Show Items:

- On Desktop: Display desktop items.
- In Stage Manager: Display desktop items when the Stage Manager feature is enabled. If you disable this **option**, the items on your desktop will be hidden—click on the desktop to reveal them whenever you want to use them.

→ Click on the "Click wallpaper to reveal desktop" drop-down menu, and pick any of the options:

- Always: Clicking your desktop's wallpaper will move all the windows out of the way to display desktop items.
- Only in Stage Manager: When Stage Manager is enabled, clicking your desktop's wallpaper will move all the windows out of the way to display desktop items.

→ Enable or deactivate Stage Manager.

→ Activate or disable the "**Show recent applications in Stage Manager**" feature. If this option is disabled, recently used applications will be hidden—simply hover the cursor to the left edge of your display to reveal them.

→ Click on the "Show windows from an app" drop-down menu, and then pick any of the options:

- One at a Time: Only display the most recently used window of an application when you switch to the application.
  To switch to another window when this option is disabled, click on the application on the left one more time to open the window.
- All at Once: Display all windows for an application when you switch to the application.

Require a password after waking your laptop

To keep your data safe when you're away from your MacBook, configure it to ask for a login code anytime it wakes from sleep.

→ Click on the Apple menu icon in the menu bar, click on the **Systems Setting** button in the menu, and then click on the **Lock Screen** button in the sidebar on the left side of the window.

→ Click the drop-down menu close to "Require a password after screensaver starts or screen is turned off," then select the amount of time that has to pass before the password is needed.

Use a screensaver

Use a screensaver to hide your desktop when you are away from your device.

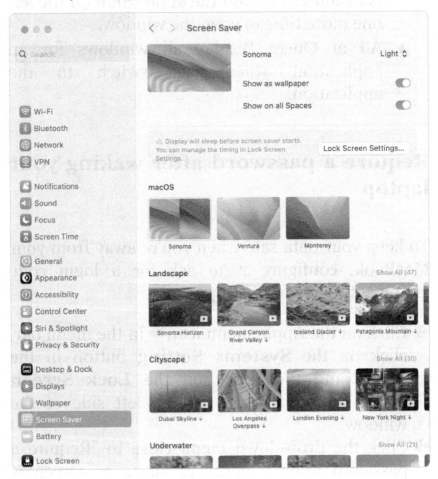

Personalize the screen saver

➜ Click on the Apple menu icon🍎, click on the **Systems Setting** button in the menu that pops-up, and then click on the **Screen Saver** button in the sidebar on the left side of the window.

➜ Choose any of the screen savers from one of the categories:
  • macOS
  • Landscapes, Earth, Underwater, & Cityscapes aerials
  • Shuffle Aerials: These pictures change at scheduled times.
  • Others

➜ Set options for your screensaver.
  For instance, you can do any of the below:
  • Activate a slow-motion aerial as your MacBook's Screensaver
  • Select a pattern to shuffle through your pictures
  • And more

Start or stop the screensaver

➜ The screensaver will automatically start when your laptop has been inactive for the period of time you selected in System Settings.
  To change how long your laptop has to stay idle before the screensaver activates, click on the

Apple menu icon in the menu bar, click on the **Systems Settings** button in the menu that appears, click on the **Lock Screen** button in the side bar, and then make the desired settings on the right side of the window.

To manually start the screensaver, simply click on the Apple menu icon in the menu bar, and then click on the **Lock Screen** button in the menu that appears.

→ Tap the trackpad, move the mouse, or press a key on the keyboard to stop the screensaver & display your desktop.

Use light or dark mode

You can use a dark or light theme for the Dock, menus bar, windows, & some applications, or have it automatically change from dark to light mode during the day.

➔ Click on the Apple menu icon🍎 in the upper left corner of your display, click on the **Systems Setting** button, and then click on the **Appearance** button in the sidebar on the left side of the window.

➔ Choose any of the options in the Appearance segment on the right side of the window(Auto, Light, or Dark)

Use Night Shift

The Night Shift feature shifts your laptop's screen to the warmer side of the colour spectrum. Warm display colours are more pleasant to look at in low-light conditions.

Set Night Shift to activate or deactivate automatically

→ Click the Apple menu icon in the menu bar, and then click on the **Systems Setting** button in the menu that pops-up.

→ Click the **Display** button in the side bar on the left side of the window

→ Click **Night Shift** on the right side of the window, click on the Schedule drop-down menu, and choose any of the options.

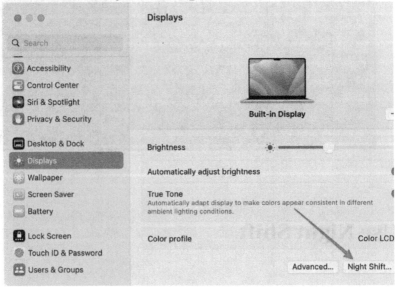

- Off
- Custom: Set the times you want the Night Shift to automatically activate or deactivate.
- Sunset to Sunrise: Use the Night Shift feature from sunset to sunrise.

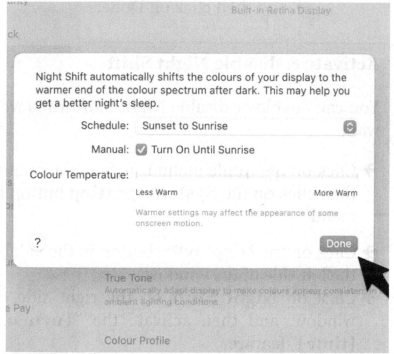

If you choose this option, your device will use your location to determine when it's night for you. You must enable Location Services to use this option; to do this, click the Apple menu icon in the menu bar, click on the **Systems Setting** button in the menu that appears, and then click on **Privacy and Security** in the sidebar on the left side of the window. Click on Location Services on the right side of the window, and then enable the Location Services feature. Scroll to Systems Service, click the **Details** button, enable Setting time zone, and then click on Done.

Activate & disable Night Shift

You can enable or disable Night Shift whenever you want.

→ Click on the Apple menu icon in the menu, and then click on the **Systems Setting** button in the menu.

→ Click on the **Display** button in the sidebar on the left side of the window

→ Click on **Night Shift** on the right side of the window, and then activate the "**Turn on till [time]**" feature.
Night Shift will remain active till the following day or till you disable it.

Tip: You can also activate or disable Night Shift through the Controls Centre. Click on the Controls

Centre icon in the upper right corner of the screen, click on Display, and then click the **Night Shift** button.

Adjust the colour temperature

➔ Click the Apple menu icon⬆ in the menu bar, and then click on the **Systems Setting** button in the menu.

➔ Click on the **Display** button in the sidebar on the left side of the window.

➔ Click on **Night Shift** on the right side of the window, and then drag the slider to the right or left end of the spectrum to adjust Night Shift's colour temperature.

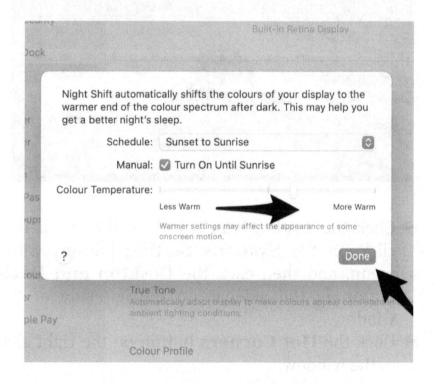

Hot Corners

The Hot Corners feature allows you to start a quick action when you hover the cursor to one of the corners of your MacBook's screen. For instance, you can start a Quick Note when you hover the cursor to the bottom right corner of your screen.

➜ Click the Apple Menu icon in the menu bar, click on the **Systems Setting** button in the menu, and then click the **Desktop and Dock** button in the sidebar on the left side of the window.
➜ Click the **Hot Corners** button on the right side of the window.

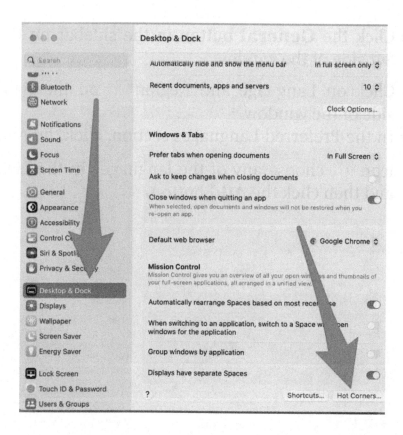

→ Click the drop-down menu for every corner you'd like to use, and then pick one of the options, like Lock Screen, Launchpad, and more.

→ Click on Done

Change your laptop's language

→ Click the Apple menu icon in the menu bar, and then click the **Systems Setting** button in the menu.

➜ Click the **General** button in the sidebar on the left side of the window

➜ Click on Language and Region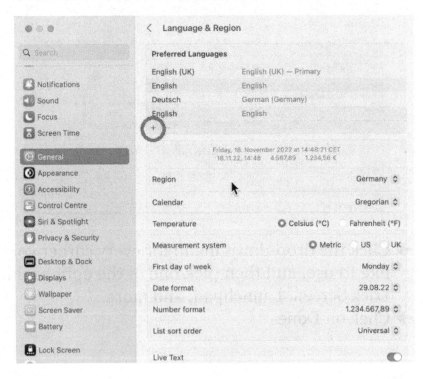 on the right side of the window.

➜ In the Preferred Languages section, click the Add icon ┼, choose any of the languages in the List, and then click the **Add** button.

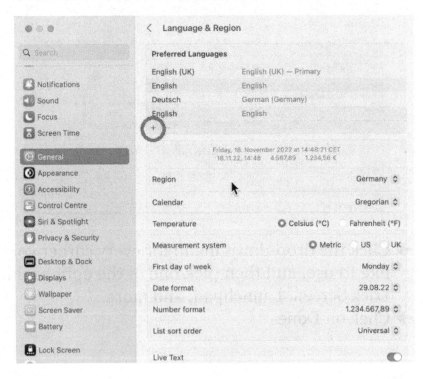

Select the language you use for each application

➔ Click on the Apple menu icon in the menu bar, click on the **Systems Setting** button in the menu, and then click on the **General** button in the sidebar on the left side of the window

➔ Click on Language and Region on the right side of the window.

➔ Head over to Applications, and then carry out any of the below:

- Pick a language for an application: Click on the Add icon ┼ , select an application and a language from the drop-down menu, and then click the **Add** button.

- Change the language for an application in the list: Pick the application, and select a language in the drop-down menu.

- Erase an application from the list: Choose the application, and then click the Delete icon ── . The application will go back to using the default language.

If the application is open, you'll need to close & reopen it for the adjustment to take effect.

Dictation

You can dictate text anywhere you can type it on your laptop.

Enable or deactivate Dictation

➔ Click the Apple menu icon in the menu bar, click the **System Settings** button in the menu,

and then click **Keyboards** in the sidebar on the left side of the window

➔ Head over to Dictation on the right side of the window, and then activate or deactivate it. If prompted, click on **Enable**.

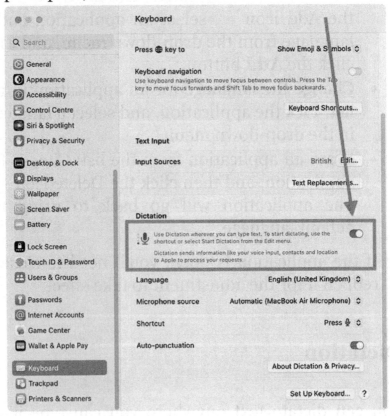

Dictate text

→ Launch any application that supports text editing on your device, then click where you want to enter text.

→ Press the Dictation key 🎤 in the FN keys row on your keyboard, or click on Edit, and then click on the **Start Dictation** button

→ Start dictating when you see the MIC icon 🎤 under or above a highlighted cursor, or when you hear the sound indicating that your MacBook is ready for dictation.

that help time our bodies' functions to optimize everything from wakefulness to digestion. Lots of exposure to sunlight helps link our sleep-wake cycle to the rising and setting of the sun. Consistency is key to developing healthy sleep patterns, and it's easy to slip out of sync in a world of constant connection, where many are used to working across multiple time zones

→ You can insert punctuation marks or add an emoji by saying the name of the punctuation mark or emoji, for example, you could say "Apostrophe" or "crying emoji"

→ When you are done, simply press the Escape button on the keyboard.

Use desktop stacks

Desktop Stacks helps to arrange your files into groups on your MacBook's desktop. Whenever you save a file to your desktop, it will be automatically added to the right stack.

Enable desktop stacks

Do any of the below on your MacBook Air:

➜ Ctrl-click the desktop, and then click the **Use Stack** option in the menu that appears

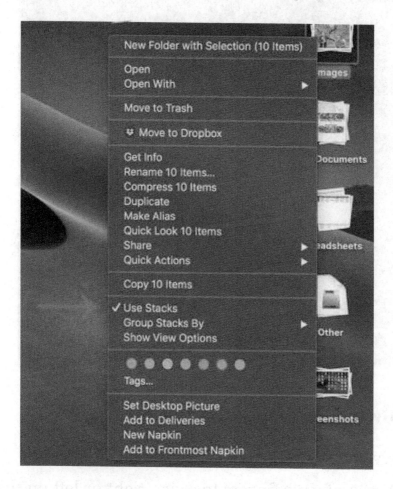

➜ Press Ctrl-Cmd-0.
➜ Click the desktop, click on **View** in the menu bar, and then click on the **Use Stacks** button in the menu that pops-up.

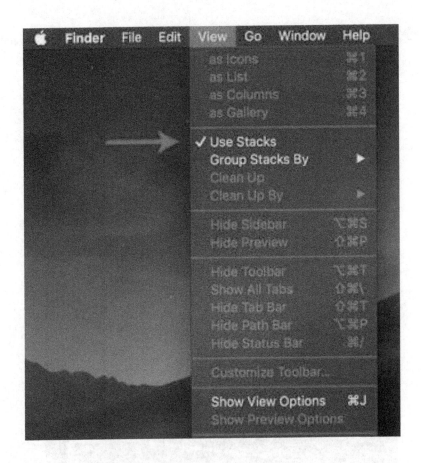

Browse files in desktop stacks

Carry out any of the below on the stack:

➔ Use 2 of your fingers to swipe right or left on the trackpad.

➔ Use a finger to swipe left or right on your Magic mouse

Expand or collapse desktop stacks

Carry out any of the below on your laptop:

→ Expand a desktop stack: Click on the stack on your Mac's desktop. After expanding the stack, double-click any of the items in the stack to open it.

→ You can close a desktop stack by clicking on its Down Arrow

Change the grouping of desktop stacks

You can change how desktop stacks are organized.

To do this, simply carry out any of the below:

→ Click the desktop, click on **View** in the upper part of your display, click on **Group Stacks By** in the menu that pops-up, and then choose one of the options.

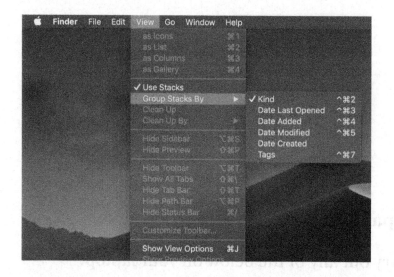

→ Ctrl-click on the desktop, select **Group Stacks By** in the menu, and then select any of the options.

Change the desktop stack appearance

You can increase icons size, change the spacing between icons, and more.

To do this, simply carry out any of the below:

→ Click the desktop, click on **View** in the upper part of your display, click on Show View Options in the menu that pops-up, and then make the desired changes.

→ Ctrl-click on the desktop, click on the **Show View Options** button in the menu that pops-up, then make the desired changes.

138

Use Live Text to interact with text in pictures

You can use the Live Text feature to copy & use the text found in pictures in the Photos app. For instance, you can copy the text on a signboard & paste it into an e-mail or document. You can look up word definitions, search the internet, and even translate text into other languages.

→ Launch the Photos application, and then open a picture that contains text.

→ Hover the cursor over the text, and then drag to select the text.
→ Carry out any of the below:

- Copy text: Press the Cmd-C keyboard shortcut or Ctrl-click on the text you selected, and then click on the **Copy** button in the menu.

- Translate text: Ctrl-click the text you selected, click on **Translate [text]**, and then pick one of the languages.

- Check the meaning of a word: Ctrl-click on what you selected, and then click **Lookup [text]**.

- Share the text: Ctrl-click on what you selected, click on the **Share** option, and then select one of the sharing methods.

- Search for the text on the Internet: Ctrl-click on what you selected, and then click on the **Search with [web searching engine]** button.

- Enter a webpage: Ctrl-click on what you selected, and then open the link in a browser.

- Contact an e-mail address: Ctrl-click on what you selected, and then write an e-mail or add the e-mail address to your Contacts list.

- Contact a phone number: Ctrl-click on what you selected, and then call the phone number, make a Face-Time call, or send a message to the phone number.

Control access to your MacBook's camera

Some applications can use your MacBook's camera to record videos and snap pictures. To choose which installed applications are allowed to use your laptop's camera, just adhere to the directions below:

➔ Click on the Apple menu icon in the menu bar, click on **Systems Setting** in the menu, and then click on the **Privacy and Security** button in the sidebar on the left side of the window.

➔ Click on Camera on the right side of the window.

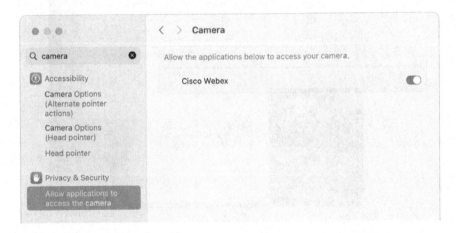

➔ Enable or deactivate access to your MacBook's camera for each application in that segment.

Quick Note

Quick Notes allows you to jot down thoughts in a note without launching the Notes app. The Quick Note will remain visible on your MacBook's display when it's open, so you can easily select & add info.

Start a Quick Note

Do any of the below to open a Quick Note:

→ Hold down the FN button or the Globe button 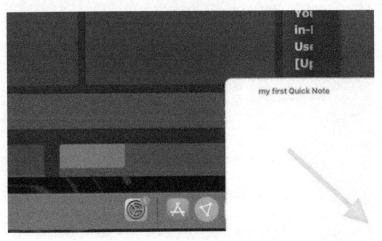 on the keyboard, and then press the **Q** key.

→ Use hot corners: Hover the pointer to the lower right edge of your MacBook's screen, and then click on the note that pops-up.

Click on the Red icon in the window to close it

Change password or user photo

→ Click the Apple menu icon in the menu bar, click the **System Settings** button in the menu, and then click on the **User and Group** button in the sidebar on the left side of the window

→ Click the Information icon ⓘ beside a user in the list on the right side of the window, and then perform any of the below:

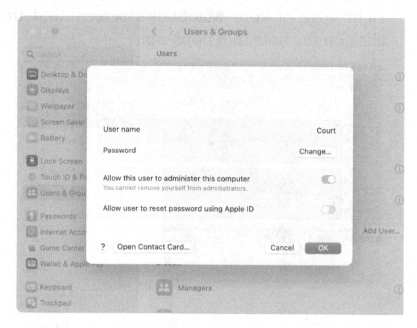

- Click a user's photo to change the login photo
- Click Change or Reset Password.

Optimize storage space

MacOS can help you free up more space on your MacBook by optimizing storage.

→ Click the Apple menu icon in the menu bar, click on **System Settings** in the menu, and then

144

click on **General** in the sidebar on the left side of the window.

➔ Click on **Storage** on the right side of the window

Recommendations

 Store in iCloud
Store all files, photos, and messages in iCloud and save space by keeping only recent files and optimized photos on this Mac when storage space is needed. Learn more...

Store in iCloud...

 Optimize Storage
Save space by automatically removing movies and TV shows that you've already watched from this Mac.

Optimize...

 Empty Trash automatically
Save space by automatically erasing items that have been in the Trash for more than 30 days. Learn more...

Turn On...

➔ Check out what macOS is recommending and decide how to optimize storage

- Store in iCloud

 Store in iCloud
Store all files, photos, and messages in iCloud and save space by keeping only recent files and optimized photos on this Mac when storage space is needed. Learn more...

- Optimize Storage

 Optimize Storage
Save space by automatically removing movies and TV shows that you've already watched from this Mac.

145

- Empty Trash automatically

 Empty Trash automatically
Save space by automatically erasing items that have been in the Trash for more than 30 days. Learn more...

Music on MacBook Air

The Apple Music application makes organizing & enjoying music easy on your device. You can check out previously played songs, lyrics for the current song, & what is next.

Click to activate or deactivate Repeat

Click to open Mini Player

Click to see the lyrics of the current song

Click to activate or deactivate Shuffle

Drag to go to a different part of the song

Drag to increase or reduce the volume

Click to see the next song

Lyrics: Click the Lyrics icon in the tools pane to see a lyrics panel for the song that is playing (if available).

146

Use Apple Music. Click the **Browse** button in the sidebar on the left side of the app window to view the latest songs & releases from Apple Music (a streaming service that's accessible for a monthly fee). Stream & download songs advertisements-free & select from dozens of playlists to find the ideal mix every time. You can even follow an artist to get new song alerts.

Listen together: With Shareplay, you can listen to songs in real-time with other people (up to Thirty-two individuals). First, bring the group together in a Face-Time call, and then click on the SharePlay icon

. To listen to songs together, hover the cursor over an album or song in the Music application, then click on **Play**. Every participant in the call will hear the same song at the same time, & have access to shared playback controls.

Purchase from the iTunes Store. If you want to have your music, click on the **iTunes Store** button in the sidebar on the left side of the window. (If you can't find iTunes Store in the side bar, click on Music in the menu bar, click on Settings in the menu, click on General, and then click on the **Show iTunes Store** button.)

Create an empty Playlist

A playlist is a collection of music & videos. You can create a playlist to suit an occasion or mood, to share with loved ones, or just organize your music library

Adhere to the directives below to create a playlist:

➜ Launch the Music application, click on **File** in the menu bar, select **New** in the menu that pops-up, and then click Playlist

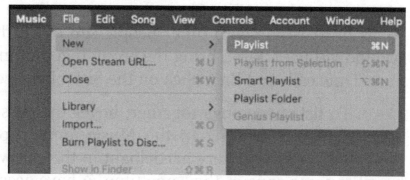

➜ Give the playlist a name, and then carry out any of the below(optional):

- Click the Add icon ⊕ above the playlist title to add an artwork, then pick one of the files from your Photos library or a location.
- Enter a description for your playlist under the title.

➜ Click on the Create button.

Add items to the playlist

➔ Launch the Music application, click on Browse, Home, or any of the other options in the Library section of the side bar to find the songs.

➔ To add an item to a playlist, perform any of the below:

• Drag an item from anywhere in your music library to one of the playlists in the Playlists section of the sidebar.

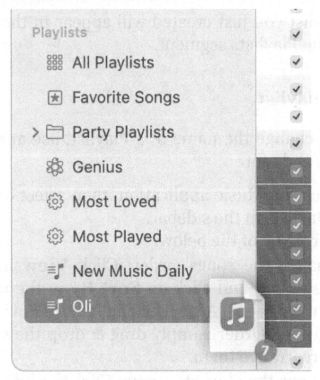

• Ctrl-click on an item, click on the **Add to Playlist** button in the menu that pops-up, and then click on one of the playlists.

149

Create a playlist of songs

➔ Launch the Music application, click on Browse, Home, or any of the other options in the Library segment of the side bar to find the songs.

➔ Select one or more songs, Ctrl-click, click on **Add to Playlists** in the menu that appears, and then click on the **New Playlist** button

The Playlist you just created will appear in the side bar, in the Playlists segment.

Edit a playlist

You can change the name of a Playlist, use another artwork, and more

➔ Launch the Music application, then select one of the playlists in the sidebar.

➔ Perform any of the below:

- Change the songs' order: Click **View** in the menu bar, and click on **Sort By** in the menu that pops-up. After clicking View> Sort By> Playlists Order, simply drag & drop the songs to rearrange them.

- Change the playlist's name: Click the Edit icon , or click on the More Options icon , then click the **Edit** button, after that, give the playlist a new name.

- Delete a song from your playlist: Select the song, and then press the **Delete** button on the keyboard.
- Change the playlist artwork: Click the Edit icon ✎ , or click on the More Options icon ••• , then click the **Edit** button, after that, pick one of the preset album covers or click on the Add icon ⊕ to add yours.
- Add recommended songs to the playlist: Click on the Add Song icon ⊕ in the Suggested Songs segment (scroll down to find it)

Delete a playlist

➜ Perform any of the below in the Music application:
- Select any of the playlists in the Playlists section of the sidebar, and then press the **Delete** button on the keyboard.
- Ctrl-click the playlist in the sidebar, and then click on the **Delete from Library** button in the menu that appears.
➜ Click on **Delete** once more.

Find which playlist a song is in

→ Enter the Music application, and then click the **Songs** button in the sidebar on the left side of the window.

→ Ctrl-click a song, and then click on the **Show in Playlist** button in the menu that appears.

The submenu will display which library & playlist category the song is in. Select the playlist from the submenu to open it.

Use AirDrop

You can use AirDrop as a means to share files with Apple devices that are near your MacBook Air (iPad, iPhone, & other Macs).

Send a file from the desktop or a Finder window: Ctrl-click the item you'd like to share, click on the **Share** button from the shortcut menu, click the **AirDrop** option, and then choose the device you'd like to send the file to.

Or, click on the Finder icon in the Dock at the lower part of your display to open a Finder window, then click the **AirDrop** button in the sidebar. When the device you want to share the file with pops up in the window, simply drag the file to it.

Send files from an application. While making use of applications that support Sharing, simply click on the Share icon in the application's tools panel, click on the **AirDrop** option, and then choose the device you'd like to send the file to.

Use Controls Centre to manage AirDrop

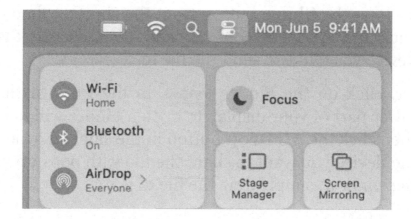

Click the Controls Centre icon in the upper right corner of your display, click the **AirDrop** button to enable or deactivate the AirDrop feature, and then select Everybody or Only Contacts to choose who you'd like to receive items from.

Receive items via AirDrop: When someone sends an item to your device via AirDrop, you can accept & save the file. When the AirDrop alert pops up, you can click on the **Accept** button, and then save the file to a folder or an app.

CHAPTER 5

SIRI

Siri makes performing tasks on your device easier. You can ask Siri questions and get quick answers; you can tell Siri to launch an application, schedule a meeting, and so on.

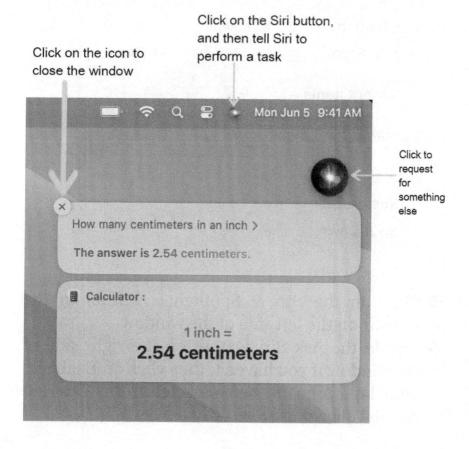

Click on the Siri button, and then tell Siri to perform a task

Click on the icon to close the window

Click to request for something else

How many centimeters in an inch ⟩

The answer is 2.54 centimeters.

Calculator :

1 inch =
2.54 centimeters

Enable Siri

→ Click on the Apple menu icon in the menu bar, and then click on the **System Settings** button in the menu.

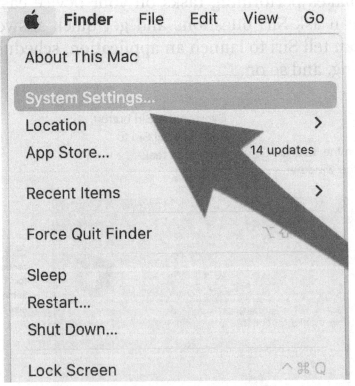

→ Click on the Siri & Spotlight button in the sidebar on the left side of the window
→ Enable the Ask Siri feature on the right side of the window if you haven't, then click on Enable Your laptop has to be connected to the Internet before you can use Siri.

➔ When asked if you'd like to improve Siri & Dictation, simply do any of the below:

- Click the **Not Now** option to not share your voice recordings
- Share voice recordings: Click the **Share Audio Recordings** option to let Apple keep audio of your Dictation & Siri interactions.

If you change your mind, just enter **System Settings**, and click on Privacy and Security in the sidebar on the left side of the window. Head over to Analytics and Improvements on the right side of the window, and then enable or deactivate Improve Siri and Dictation.

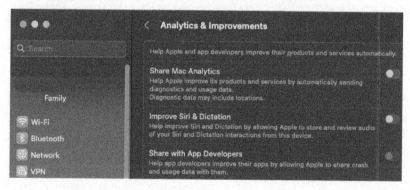

➔ Carry out any of the below:

- Use "Siri" or "Hey Siri": Enable the "Listen for" feature or pick a phrase you can say to activate Siri. When this option is enabled and you activate the **"Allow Siri when locked"** feature, you can also summon Siri even when your laptop is locked.

- Create a shortcut: Click on the "Keyboard Shortcut" drop-down menu, and then select any of the shortcuts to summon Siri or create one for yourself.

Tip: You can long-press the MIC button 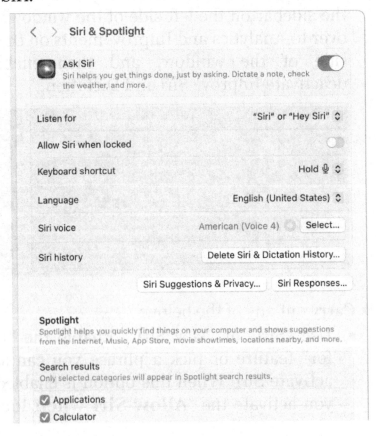 in the FN keys row on your keyboard to summon Siri.

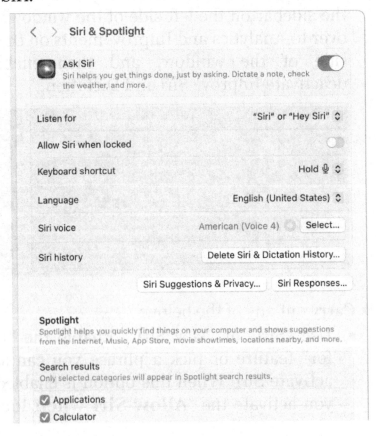

- Change Siri's Language or Voice: Click on the Language drop-down menu, and then select any of the available languages. To hear a preview of Siri's voice, click on the Select button beside **Siri Voice**, and then choose any of the Voice Varieties & options
- Mute Siri: Click on Siri's Response, and then disable **Voice feedback—** you will see Siri's response in the Siri window.
- Display Siri's Response on your screen: Click on Siri's Response, and then enable "Always show Siri captions."
- Display what you're saying on the screen: Click on Siri's Response, and then enable the **Always Show Speech** option.

Note: To add Siri to the menu bar, open **System Settings**, and then click Controls Centre⊟ in the sidebar on the left side of the window. Head over to the **Menu Bar Only** section on the right side of the window, and then select the **Show in the Menu Bar** option beside Siri.

Summon Siri

Your MacBook has to have internet connection before you can use Siri.

➔ Carry out any of the below to summon Siri:

- Long-press the Microphone button 🎤 in the FN keys row on your keyboard or use the keyboard shortcut you created.

- Click on the Siri button ⚫ in the upper right corner of your screen.

- Say "Siri" or "Hey Siri" if you've enabled the "**Listen for**" feature in System Settings

➔ Request for something—for instance, ask Siri to set a meeting at 12 or ask for the time.

Disable Siri

➔ Enter **System Settings**, and then click the Siri & Spotlight ⚫ button in the sidebar

➔ Disable the Ask Siri feature on the right side of the window

CHAPTER 6

ICLOUD

iCloud keeps your important data, (such as your documents, pictures, videos, etc.) safe, & accessible across all your Apple devices. iCloud provides an e-mail account & 5GB of free storage space. You can upgrade to iCloud+ to get more storage & features.

To get started, sign in with your Apple ID to configure iCloud. After logging in, basic iCloud features (such as iCloud Photo, iCloud Drive, etc.) are automatically configured. You can activate or deactivate these features & change the settings at any time.

Here are some ways to use iCloud on your MacBook:

→ ICloud Photos keeps your videos & images safe and makes your pictures and videos available on all your devices & the iCloud.com site.
→ Keep your files safe in iCloud Drive.
→ With the Family Sharing feature, you can share applications, subscriptions, songs, books, and so on with your family members
→ ICloud Private Relay: Hide your IP address & browsing activities in the Safari browser &

encrypt your Internet traffic so that nobody, including Apple, can know who you are or what sites you are visiting.

→ The Hide My E-mail feature keeps your e-mail address private by creating random & unique addresses that are forwarded to your personal inbox so you don't have to share your real email address when filling out forms online or registering for newsletters.

→ iCloud Keychain: Keep your passcodes, credit cards, and so on safe in iCloud.

→ And lots more.

Manage iCloud storage

You get 5GB of free storage after logging in with your Apple ID & turning on iCloud. To increase your storage space, simply upgrade to iCloud+

→ Click the Apple menu icon in the menu bar, click on the **System Settings** button in the menu, and then click on [your name] in the sidebar on the left side of the window.
If you can't find your name there, just click on **Sign in to your Apple ID** to insert your Apple ID details or create an Apple ID.

➔ Click on **iCloud** on the right side of the window, click the **Manage** button, and then carry out any of the below:

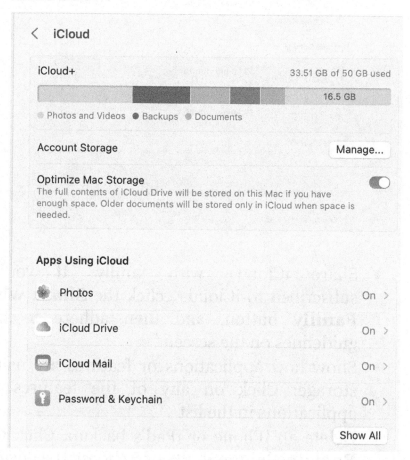

- Increase or reduce the storage space: click on Change your Storage Plan or Add Storage, and then adhere to the guidelines on your display.

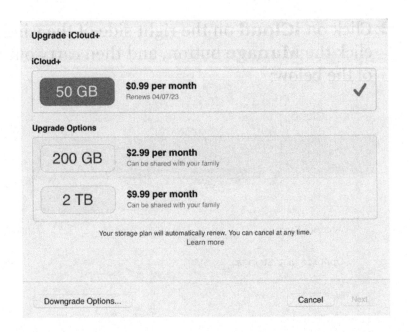

- Share iCloud+ with family: If you've subscribed to iCloud+, click the **Share with Family** button, and then adhere to the guidelines on the screen.
- Show how applications or features are using storage: Click on any of the features or applications in the list.
- Delete an iPhone or iPad's backup: Click the **Backups** button in the list, choose the device, and then click on Remove — in the backups list segment.
- Disable Siri & delete Siri-related data: Click on the Siri button in the list, and then click on Disable & Delete

➜ Click the Done button.

Keep files in iCloud Drive

Keep your files safe & organized in iCloud Drive.

Set up iCloud Drive

Adhere to the directives below to configure iCloud Drive (if you haven't):

→ Click the Apple menu icon in the menu bar, click on the **System Settings** button in the menu, and then click on [your name] in the sidebar on the left side of the window.
If you can't find your name there, just click on **Sign in to your Apple ID** to insert your Apple ID details or create an Apple ID.

→ Click on **iCloud** on the right side of the window, click the **iCloud Drive** button, and then enable Sync this Mac.

→ Click the Done button.

Store files in your Documents & Desktop folders in iCloud Drive

You can configure your MacBook Air to automatically save all files in your Documents & Desktop folders to iCloud Drive. So you can save files wherever you usually save them, and they'll be available on all your Apple devices & the iCloud.com website.

→ Click the Apple menu icon🍎 in the menu bar, click on the **System Settings** button in the menu, and then click on [your name] in the sidebar on the left side of the window.
If you can't find your name there, just click on **Sign in to your Apple ID** to insert your Apple ID details or create an Apple ID.

→ Click on **iCloud** on the right side of the window, click on the **iCloud Drive** button, then ensure iCloud Drive is enabled.

→ Activate Desktop and Document Folders

→ Click the Done button.

After turning on Desktop and Document Folders, the Desktop & Document folders will be moved to iCloud Drive. They'll also be available in the iCloud segment of the Finder sidebar on your laptop, and the Files application on your iPad or iPhone (if you have one).

Use iCloud Photos

When you turn on iCloud Photos, all your videos & pictures in the Photos library will be saved in iCloud, so they can be easily accessed from all your Apple devices & the iCloud.com website.

Any new videos & pictures that you save in the Photos app will appear on all your devices that have iCloud Photos activated.

Getting Started

Do the following before setting up iCloud Photos:

➔ Ensure your MacBook Air and other Apple devices have been updated to the latest OS (macOS, iPadOS, and others) versions.
➔ Log in with your Apple ID: If you haven't logged in with your Apple ID, enter **System Settings**, click on **Sign in to Apple ID** in the sidebar, then enter your Apple ID details or create an Apple ID. Click on the **iCloud** button on the right side of the window, click the **Photos** option in the applications list, and then activate Sync Mac.

Activate iCloud Photos

➔ Launch the Photos application, click on **Photos** in the menu bar, click on **Settings** in the menu that appears, and then click on **iCloud**.

➜ Tick the iCloud Photo checkbox

iCloud

⚙️ General ☁️ iCloud 👥 Shared Library

☑️ **iCloud Photos**

Automatically upload and store all your photos and videos in iCloud so you can access them from any of your devices and on the web.

  Download Originals to this Mac

  Store original photos and videos on this Mac. Choose this option if you want to access full-resolution versions of your entire library, even when offline.

  ⦿ **Optimize Mac Storage**

  If your Mac is low on space, full-resolution photos and videos are automatically replaced with smaller, device-sized versions. Full-resolution versions can be downloaded from iCloud anytime.

☑️ **Shared Albums**

Create albums to share with other people, and subscribe to other people's shared albums.

➜ Select any of the options below:

- **Optimize this MacBook's Storage**

  ⦿ Optimize Mac Storage

  If your Mac is low on space, full-resolution photos and videos are automatically replaced with smaller, device-sized versions. Full-resolution versions can be downloaded from iCloud anytime.

- **Download Originals to MacBook**

  Download Originals to this Mac

  Store original photos and videos on this Mac. Choose this option if you want to access full-resolution versions of your entire library, even when offline.

The first time you enable iCloud Photos, it may take some time to upload your files to iCloud. You can keep using the Photos applications while your files are being uploaded.

To sync iCloud photos across all your Apple devices, use the same Apple ID to activate iCloud Photos across all your Apple devices.

Stop using iCloud Photos on your laptop

You can disable iCloud Photos on your MacBook Air to stop videos & pictures from being updated between your MacBook and your other Apple devices.

→ Launch the Photos application on your MacBook Air, click on **Photos** in the menu bar, click on **Settings** in the menu that appears, and then click on **iCloud**.
→ Unselect the iCloud Photo check box
→ Click the **Download** button to download videos & pictures from iCloud to your device, or click the **Remove from Mac** option to remove files that haven't been fully downloaded.

After disabling iCloud Photo on your device, your photos library will remain in iCloud & available to your other Apple devices that have iCloud Photos turned on.

Stop using iCloud Photos on all your Apple devices

→ Click the Apple menu icon in the menu bar, click on the **System Settings** button in the menu, and then click on [your name] in the sidebar on the left side of the window. If you can't find your name there, just click on **Sign in to your Apple ID** to insert your Apple ID details or create an Apple ID.

→ Click on **iCloud** on the right side of the window

→ Click on the Manage option, click on Photos, and then click on "**Turn Off & Delete**"

NOTE: If you disable iCloud Photos on all your devices, your files will be deleted from iCloud after **30** days, and you'll not be able to get the files back unless you click on the **Undo Delete** button before that time.

CHAPTER 7

SAFARI APP

You can use the Safari browser to surf through the web, visit sites, translate webpages, etc.

Visit a site

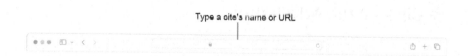

→ Launch the Safari application, and then type the URL or name of the website in the search box.

Suggestions will appear as you type.

→ Choose one of the suggestions or press the Return key on your keyboard to visit the address you entered.

Add bookmarks

Bookmarks are links to websites that you save so you can easily visit the websites later.

→ Launch the Safari application, and then visit the site you'd like to bookmark.

→ Click on the Share icon in the tools panel, and then click on the **Add Bookmarks** button.

→ Pick where you want to add the bookmark & change the bookmark's name (optional).

- Add this page: Click on the drop-down menu and pick any of the folders.

- Change the bookmark's name: Type a short name.

- Add description: Type more info about the site.

→ Click on the **Add** button.

Find your bookmarks

→ Launch the Safari application, click on the Sidebar icon in the tools panel at the upper part of the window, and then click the **Bookmarks** button.

→ Type the name of the bookmark in the sidebar's search box.
Drag down to bring out the search box (if you can't find it).

Use a bookmark

→ Launch the Safari application, click on the Sidebar icon in the tools panel at the upper part of the window, and then click the **Bookmarks** button
Or, click on the **Bookmarks** button in the menu bar, and then click on **Show Bookmarks** in the menu that appears.

→ Click any of the bookmarks in the sidebar.

Manage bookmarks

→ Launch the Safari application, click on the Sidebar icon in the tools panel at the upper part of the window, and then click the **Bookmarks** button

→ Ctrl-click on one of the bookmarks or folders
→ Pick from the available options in the menu that appear to do any of the below:
- Change the name of or edit a folder or bookmark.
- Create a bookmark folder
- Change the site address (URL).
- Delete or copy a folder or bookmark.

To change the description of a bookmark, double-click a folder on the sidebar, then ctrl-click on the item, and choose the **Edit Descriptions** option from the menu that appears.

Use tabs

Avoid cluttering your desktop with many windows when you are browsing or researching a topic online. Instead, you can browse multiple web pages in a Safari window using tabs.

Preview a tab

Simply hover the cursor over the tab in the Safari application.

Open a new tab

➔ Launch the Safari application, and then click the Add Tab icon ➕ in the tools panel at the upper part of your display.

Open a page in a new tab

Carry out any of the below in the Safari application:

➔ Cmd-click on a link on a page.

➔ Cmd-click on the Forward icon ❯ or the Back icon ❮ to go to the next or previous page in another tab.

➔ Write in the Search bar, and then Command-click any of the search suggestions, or press the Cmd-Return keyboard combination.

Open a tab in another window

While using the Safari application, click on the **Window** button in the menu bar, and then click on **Move Tab to a New Window** in the menu that appears.

Reopen a recently closed tab

While using the Safari application, click the **History** button in the menu bar, click on **Recently**

Closed in the menu that appears, and then select the website you'd like to reopen.

You can also reopen a closed window or tab.

Safari Reader

Use Reader's View to view a webpage without advertisements, navigations, or any other item that could cause distraction.

View articles in Reader's view

→ While on a webpage in the Safari application, click on the Reader icon ⬜ in the Search box.

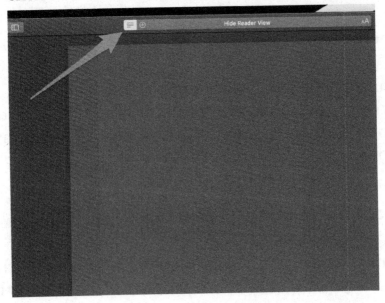

The icon will only appear if the website has content that Reader's view can show.

→ To exit Reader's View, click on the Reader button one more time or press the Esc key on your keyboard.

Change a webpage's format

→ While viewing an article in Reader's view in the Safari application, click the Format icon AA in the search box.

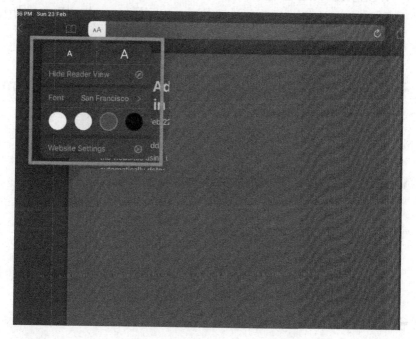

→ Carry out any of the below to change the settings:
   • Pick any of the font sizes.

- Pick one of the background colours.
- Select a font.

Translate a webpage

If you come across a website that's in a language you do not understand, you can use the Safari application to translate the text.

→ Launch the Safari application, then visit the website you'd like to translate
If the page is translatable, you'll see the Translate icon in the search bar.

→ Click the Translation icon , and then pick any of the languages.

View items you downloaded

→ Click the Downloads icon in the upper part of the Safari window.
You won't see the icon if the download list is empty.

→ Carry out any of the below:

- Pause a download: Click the Stop icon close to the filename in the download list to pause

178

what you're downloading. Click the Continue icon to resume.

- Look for a downloaded item on your laptop: Click on the Magnifier icon close to the file's name in the download list.
Note: To change where downloaded files are stored on your device, click the **Safari** button in the menu bar, click on **Settings** in the menu that appears, click the **General** button, then click the "**File download location**" drop-down menu, and then choose one of the available locations
- Clear the download list: Click the **Clear** button in the download list. To remove an item, Ctrl-click the item, then click the **Remove From List** button in the menu that appears.

Save a picture from a website

→ Ctrl-click on the picture on the webpage to show the shortcut menu
→ Click on the Add Image to Photos, Save Image As, or the Save Image to Downloads button.

Print or create a PDF file of a page

→ While using the Safari application, click on the **File** button in the menu bar, and then click on **Print** in the menu that appears.

→ Click on the options drop-down menu (in the separators bar), select Safari, and set the page printing option.
If you can't find the options drop-down menu in a separators bar close to the page's preview, simply click on the **Show Details** button at the bottom of the Print dialog.
To create a PDF file of the page, simply click on the **PDF** button at the bottom of the dialog, then adhere to the directives on your display.

Interact with text in an image in the Safari browser

You can highlight the text in a picture, and then interact with them in many ways, for instance, if an image shows an address or e-mail address, you can use the text to get more information about the location in the Maps app or write an e-mail.

→ Navigate to the picture that has text in it in the Safari application.

→ Hover the cursor over the text, and then drag to highlight the text.

→ Ctrl-click the highlighted text to display the Options menu.

→ Carry out any of the below:

- Copy text: Click on **Copy** and then paste it into a document, or application.

- Find the meaning of a word: Click the Lookup option.

- Translate text: Click on the **Translate [text]** button, and then choose any of the languages.

- Share the text: Click the **Share** option, and then use any of the sharing methods to send it.

- Search for the text on the Internet: Click on **Search with [web searching engine]**.

- Go to a site: Open the link in the browser.

- Contact a phone number: Choose to call the phone number, start a call, or send a message to the phone number.

- See a map: Launch the Maps application to see a map of the address.

- Compose an e-mail address: Choose to write an e-mail or add the e-mail address to your Contacts list.

Change your browser's homepage

The homepage is the webpage that appears anytime you open a new tab or window.

→ While using the Safari application, click on **Safari** in the menu bar, click on **Settings** in the menu that appears, and then click on the **General** tab.

→ Type the website address in the box next to **Homepage**. To use the webpage you are currently viewing, click on the Set to Current Page button.

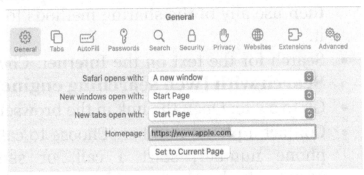

→ Select when your home page appears.

- Open a new window with your home page: Click on the **New Window open with** drop-down menu, and then pick the **Homepage** option.

- Open a new tab with your home page: Click on the **New tab open with** drop-down menu, then pick the **Homepage** option.

Allow or block pop-ups on a site

Pop-ups can be useful or annoying. Some sites require you to permit pop-ups. For instance, a bank's site may display your monthly bank statement in a pop-up. Other sites may fill your display with pop-up advertisements.

To allow or block pops-up, simply adhere to the directives below:

→ Visit the website in the Safari application.

→ Click on **Safari** in the menu bar, click on **Settings** in the menu that appears, and then click on the **Websites** tab.

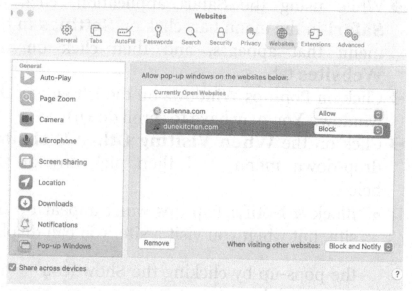

→ Click on Pop-ups Windows on the left side of the window (scroll down, if necessary).

➔ In the drop-down menu for the site, pick any of the below:
- Block & Notify: Pop-ups won't appear on the site, but when you visit a site, you can display the pops-up by clicking the Show icon 🗗 in the Search box.
- Blocked: Pop-ups will not appear on the site.
- Allow: Pop-ups will appear on the site.

Allow or block pop-ups on all sites

➔ While using the Safari application, click on **Safari** in the menu bar, click on **Settings** in the menu that appears, and then click on the **Websites** tab.

➔ Click on Pop-ups Windows on the left side of the window. (You may have to scroll down)

➔ Click on the **When Visiting Other Websites** drop-down menu, and then pick any of the below:
- Block & Notify: Pop-ups won't appear on the site, but when you visit a site, you can display the pops-up by clicking the Show icon 🗗 in the Search box.
- Blocked: Pop-ups will not appear on the sites.
- Allow: Pop-ups will appear on the sites.

Clear cookies

You can view all sites that have saved cookies & site data on your device, and you can delete some or all of them.

→ While using the Safari application, click on **Safari** in the menu bar, click on **Settings** in the menu that appears, and then click on the **Privacy** tab.

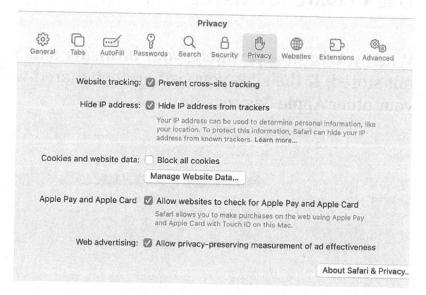

→ Click on the **Manage Websites data** button.
→ Choose the sites, and then click the Remove or Remove All button.

Clear your browsing history

➜ While using the Safari application, click on **History** in the menu bar, click on **Clear History** in the menu that appears, and then click on the drop-down menu.
➜ Select how much data you want to erase.

Use Private browsing

When you browse privately, your browsing data are not stored, & the sites you visit are not shared with your other Apple devices.

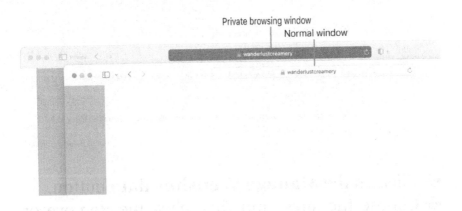

Private browsing window
Normal window

➜ While using the Safari application, click on **File** in the menu bar, and then click on **New Private**

Window in the menu that appears, or go to a private window that has already been opened.

The search box of a private window is usually dark

➔ Visit sites as you normally would

To leave Private browsing, simply close the window, and switch to a normal window or click **File** in the menu bar, and then click on **New Window** in the menu that appears to open a normal window

Lock private windows in the Safari browser

Private Browsing Is Locked

Touch ID or enter the password for the user "   " to view locked tabs.

Enter password

You can lock all your private windows and configure your device to ask for your password or Touch ID whenever you want to access them.

Allow private windows to be locked

While using the Safari application, click on **Safari** in the menu bar, click on **Settings** in the menu that appears, click on the **Privacy** tab, then select "Require a password to view locked tabs" and "Require Touch ID to view locked tabs."

Deselect the options above if you want private browsing windows to always stay unlocked.

Lock private windows

While using the Safari application, click on **Window** in the menu bar, and then click on **Lock All Private Window** in the menu that appears

CHAPTER 8

MAIL

Use the Mail application to manage all your e-mail accounts.

Add an email account

Adhere to the guidelines below to add your existing e-mail accounts to the Mail app.

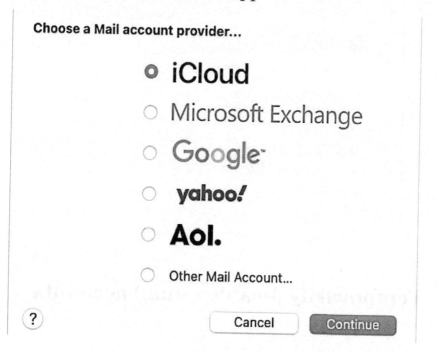

➜ When you launch the Mail app for the 1st time, you'll be prompted to add an account. Pick one of the account types (like, iCloud, Google for Gmail, AOL, and so on), or the **Other Mail Account** option, then enter your account details

➜ To add more accounts, launch the Mail app, click on **Mail** in the menu bar, click on the **Add Accounts** button in the menu that appears, select any of the account types, and then enter your account details. Ensure you select the checkbox for the account type.

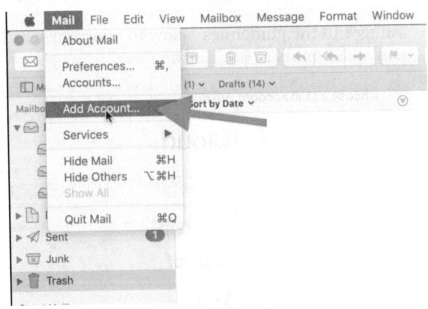

Temporarily disable e-mail accounts

You can temporarily deactivate an e-mail account to stop receiving messages from the account. You can reactivate the account at any time.

→ While using the Mail application, click on **Mail** in the menu bar, click on **Settings** in the menu that appears, and then click on the **Accounts** button.

→ Select the account you'd like to deactivate, and then unselect the "Enable this account" checkbox.

To reactivate the account, simply select the "Enable this account" checkbox.

Remove email accounts from Mail

When you remove an e-mail account, the account's messages will be erased from your laptop.

→ While using the Mail application, click on **Mail** in the menu bar, click on the **Settings** button in the menu that appears, and then click on Accounts.

→ Choose any of your accounts, and then click on the Remove icon —

Note: If other applications are also using the account, you'll be asked to remove the account in Internet Account settings. Enter Systems Setting, click on Internet Accounts, then select the account and deactivate Mail.

Compose & send an e-mail

➜ Launch the Mail application, and then click the Compose Email icon ☑ in the Mail tools panel.

➜ In the To field of the message, enter the e-mail address of the person(s) you want to send the message to.
While typing, your device will display email addresses that you've used before in the Mail application or that it found in the Contacts application
To use another field, like Priority or Bcc, click the Header icon ▭∨, then click a field.

➜ If you have more than one email address registered in the Mail application, you can pick the address you want to send the e-mail from. To do this, simply hover the cursor over the From field in the e-mail, click on the drop-down menu that pops-up, and then choose any of your e-mail addresses

➜ Type the subject of the e-mail in the Subject field and then add your message in the Message field (under the Subject field).
You can carry out any of the below:

- Click the Formatting icon 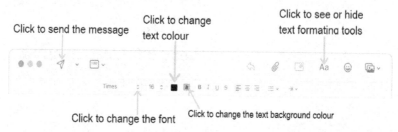 to change the styles, fonts, and more.

Click to send the message

Click to change
text colour

Click to see or hide
text formating tools

Times   16   **a** B *I* U S ≡ ≡ ≡ ≡˅ ✏˅

Click to change the font   Click to change the text background colour

- Click the Emoji button ☺ to insert symbols & emoji.
- Click on the Add Attachment button✐ or the Photos button 🖼˅ to add pictures or documents.

→ When you're done, click the Send icon ◁ .

Use the Send Later feature

Click the drop-down menu beside the Send icon ◁ in an e-mail, and then choose one of the available options.

You can find the e-mail in the Send Later mailbox in the sidebar.

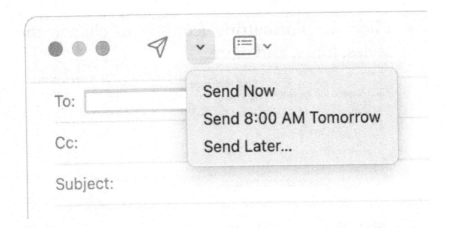

To adjust the scheduled time for the e-mail, simply open the Send Later mailbox, double-click the e-mail, and then click on the **Edit** button.

To prevent the e-mail from sending, simply open the Send Later mailbox, select the e-mail, and then click on the Trash icon 🗑.

Unsend an email

If you made a mistake in your e-mail or sent the wrong email, you have about 10 seconds (you can increase the amount of time) to unsend the e-mail.

→ After sending the email in the Mail application, click on the **Undo Send** button in the lower part of the side bar within ten seconds of sending the email.

Click to Undo Send.

Or, click the **Edit** button in the menu bar, and then choose the **Undo** option in the menu that appears.

Note: To change how long you have to unsend an email or to disable the **Undo Send** feature, click on **Mail** in the menu bar, choose the **Settings** option in the menu that appears, click on **Composing**, click on the "Undo send delay" drop-down menu, and then choose any of the options.

Redirect an email

You can redirect an email you received by mistake to the intended recipient.

→ Launch the Mail application, then select the message you'd like to redirect

→ Click on the **Message** button in the menu bar, and then click on the **Redirect** button

➔ Address the email, and then click on the Send icon ◁

The recipient will only see the address of the original sender, and any reply the recipient sends will go directly to the original sender.

Read emails from a specific email account or mailbox

Carry out any of the below in the Mail application:

➔ View emails from a mailbox: Click on the Mailbox in the sidebar.

➔ View emails from a specific e-mail account: Click the arrow beside a mailbox (for instance, inbox) in the sidebar, and then choose one of your email accounts.

Reply or forward an email

1. Launch the Mail application, then select any of the messages from the messages list.
2. Hover the cursor over the message header, and then click any of the icons below:
   - The Reply icon ↰ to reply to the sender only.

- The Reply All icon ↞ to reply to the sender & others.
- The Forward icon ↪ to pick new recipients.
3. Type your response.
4. Click the Send Email icon ◁ when you are done.

Receive reminders to follow up on e-mails with no response

If you send an email and don't get a reply within 3 days, the message will automatically go to the top of your inbox so you don't forget to follow up.

To enable or disable this feature, click on **Mail** in the menu bar, click on **Settings** in the menu that appears, click the **General** button, then select or unselect the check box close to **"Enable message follow up suggestion"**.

Use the Remind Me feature

If you do not have time to respond to an e-mail at the moment, you can set a date & time to receive a reminder & push the message back to the top of your inbox.

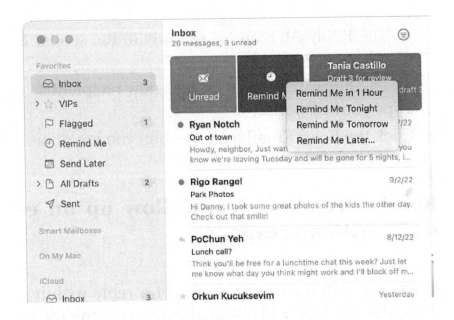

→ Launch the Mail application, select any of the messages, use 2 fingers to swipe right on your Mouse or trackpad, and then click on the **Remind Me** option from the menu. Or just Ctrl-click the message.

→ Pick any of the available options.
If you picked the **Remind Me Later** option, set when you'd like to be reminded.

Print emails

→ Launch the Mail application, and then select 1 or more messages

→ Click on the **File** button in the menu bar, and then click on **Print** in the menu that appears.

Delete emails

1. Launch the Mail application, and then select 1 or more messages.

2. Click on the Trash button 🗑 in the tools panel or hover the cursor over the message's header, and then click on **Delete** when it appears.

Search for emails

→ Launch the Mail application, and then type a phrase that can be found in the e-mail in the search box at the upper part of the window (if you can find the search box, just click on the Search icon 🔍 in the tools panel).

→ Press the Return button on your keyboard and choose any of the results

→ When you are done, click the Clear icon ⊗ in the search box.

Use Mail Privacy Protection

The Mail application can protect your privacy. The e-mail messages you receive may contain extended content that allows the sender to collect data when you view the message, such as when and how often you view it, your IP address, and other info. The Mail Privacy Protection setting stops the sender from getting any information from you.

→ Launch the Mail application, and then click on Mail in the menu bar, click on **Settings** in the menu that appears, and then click on the **Privacy** button.

→ Choose **Protect mail activity**.

CHAPTER 9
APPLE PAY

You can use Apple Pay to make safe & private purchases on your MacBook Air.

Configure Apple Pay on your device

→ Click the Apple menu icon in the menu bar, click on the **Systems Setting** button in the menu, and then click the **Wallet and Apple Pay** button in the sidebar on the left side of the window.

→ Click the **Add Card** button.
  If you've not signed in with your Apple ID on your device, you'll be asked to log in. After signing in, click on the **Wallet & Apple Pay** button in the sidebar.
→ Insert payment details.
  • Add a new card: Use your laptop's front camera to scan your card, and then adhere to the directives on your display. Or click on the **Enter Card Details Manually** button, then provide any required info.

Change wallet and Apple Pay settings

→ Click the Apple menu icon in the menu bar, click on the **Systems Setting** button in the menu, and then click the **Wallet and Apple Pay** button in the sidebar on the left side of the window (scroll down, if necessary).
→ Carry out any of the below:
  ➢ Add card: You can use your MacBook's front camera to scan your card or enter your card details manually. Click on the **Add Card** button, and then adhere to the guidelines on your display.
  ➢ Default card: Pick any of your cards to use it as your primary card for payment.

- ➤ Apple Pay & privacy
- ➤ Email
- ➤ Shipping Address
- ➤ Phone

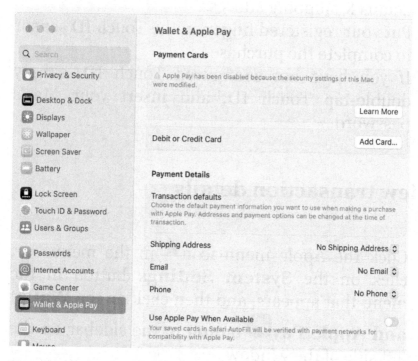

To remove a card from Apple Pay, click the card, and then click the **Remove Card** button.

Make payments with Apple Pay

You can use Apple Pay to make payments in the Safari browser or other applications.

→ When checking out from an online store, click the **Apple Pay** button.

You can change the card you want to use to make payments. You can also change your contact details & shipping address.

→ Put your registered finger on the Touch ID sensor to complete the purchase.

If you have not configured Touch ID, simply double-tap Touch ID, and insert your Mac's password.

View transaction details

→ Click the Apple menu icon in the menu bar, click on the **System Settings** button in the menu that appears, and then click on the **Wallet and Apple Pay** button in the sidebar on the left side of the window.

→ Click any of the cards, and then activate "Show Transaction Notifications".

The last transactions related to the selected card will be displayed.

CHAPTER 10

FACETIME

Use the FaceTime application to make voice & video calls from your laptop to other people.

FaceTime requirements

You have to meet the following requirements before you can make video & voice calls with FaceTime:

→ Connect your laptop to the Internet
→ Log in to FaceTime using your Apple ID

Log in to FaceTime on your device

The first time you launch the FaceTime application on your laptop, you will be prompted to log in.

→ Simply fill in your Apple ID details in the appropriate boxes.
→ Click on "Next" to sign in. FaceTime would be automatically activated on your device.

Sign out of or turn off FaceTime

Launch the FaceTime application, and then do any of the below:

→ Log out of Face-Time: Click on **FaceTime** in the menu bar, click on **Settings** in the menu, click on the **General** button, and then click on Sign Out.

→ Turn off FaceTime: Click on **FaceTime** in the menu bar, and click on **Turn Off FaceTime** in the menu that appears. To reactivate FaceTime, simply click on the **Turn On** button.

Make a FaceTime call

→ Launch the FaceTime application, and then click on the **New FaceTime** button.

→ Do any of the below to add callers to the New FaceTime window:

- Insert the number or e-mail address of the individual you would like to call. You may have to press the Return button on your keyboard.
- If the individual is on your contacts list, you can simply type the name of the individual or choose one of the contacts in the Suggested section.

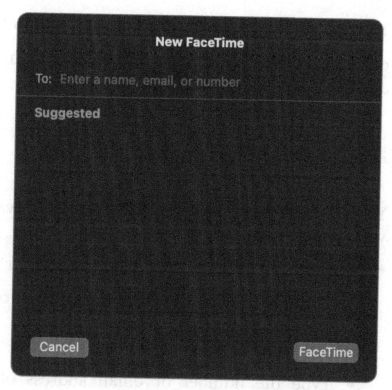

→ To make a group call, simply repeat the steps above till you add all the participants (you can add up to 32 individuals).

→ Click on the **FaceTime** button to make a video call. To make a voice call, click on the drop-down arrow ∨ , and then click on the **FaceTime Audio** button. Click on the Video icon◼ to switch to a FaceTime video call.

To send an audible notification to callers who have not yet joined the call, click the Sidebar icon , and then click on the **Ring** button.

Add more individuals to the call

You can add more individuals to the call, even if you're not the one who started the call.

→ While on a FaceTime call, click the Sidebar icon , and then click the **Add People** button or the Add People icon .

→ Carry out any of the below:

- Type the number or email address of the individual you would like to call. You may have to press the Return button on your keyboard.

- If the individual is on your contacts list, you can simply type the name of the individual or choose one of the contacts in the Suggested section
  To add many individuals at the same time, simply fill in each person's contact details in the To field.

→ Click on the **Add** button

End a call

You can do any of the below to end a FaceTime call:

→ End a voice call: Click the End call icon .
→ End a video call: Hover the cursor over the window, and then click on the End icon .

Accept a Face-Time call

→ Do any of the below when an alert pops-up on your MacBook's screen:
  ➢ Click the **Accept** button to take the call.
  ➢ Accept a video call as a voice call: Click the Arrow ∨ beside Accept, and then Pick the **Answer as Audio** option.
  ➢ Accept an incoming call & end the current call: Click on the **End and Accept** button.
  ➢ Accept an incoming call & put the current call on Hold: Click the **Hold and Accept** button.
  ➢ Join a Face-Time Group call: Click on the **Join** button, and then click on the Join icon in the Face-Time app window.

Reject Face-Time calls

| Jasmine | Accept |
| FaceTime Audio | Decline ⌄ |

→ Do any of the below when an alert pops-up on your MacBook's screen:

> Click on the **Decline** button to reject a call.

> Decline the call & send a message or set a reminder to call back later: Click on the Arrow ⌄ close to Decline, choose any of the options, and then adhere to the instructions on the display.

Create & share a link to a Face-Time call

You can create a Face-Time call link & share it with others.

→ Launch the FaceTime application, and do any of the below:

• Create a link to a call: Click the **Create Link** button.

• Create a link to the current call: Click the FaceTime Sidebar icon ▱, and then click the **Create Link** button.

- Share a link to a previous call: Click the Information icon 🛈 , and then click the Share icon 📤.

→ Share the link with any of the available sharing methods.

To join a call from a FaceTime link, simply click or touch the link, and then adhere to the onscreen directives to start or join the call.

Allow callers to join Face-Time calls

A badge will appear on the FaceTime Sidebar icon ⊟ when someone is requesting to join the call.

→ While on a FaceTime call, click the Sidebar icon when you see a badge ⧉ on it.

→ Carry out any of the below:

  ➢ Click the Approve icon ✅ to let the individual in.

  ➢ Click the Decline icon ❌ to decline the individual's offer

To prevent the FaceTime app from playing a sound anytime someone joins the call, click the FaceTime Sidebar icon ⊟ , and then click the **Silence Join Request** button.

Delete a FaceTime link

➔ In the FaceTime application, check the calls list to see the call you made with a Face-Time link

➔ Click the Details icon ⓘ, and then click the **Delete Link** button

Use SharePlay to share your screen in a FaceTime call

The SharePlay feature allows you to share what's on your screen with other participants of the call. You can show applications, webpages, & more during a video call in the FaceTime application.

➔ While making a FaceTime call, launch the application you'd like to share in the video call.

➔ Click the FaceTime Video icon in the upper part of your screen.

➔ Click on the Share Display icon , and then carry out any of the below:
  ➢ Share an app window: Click on the **Window** button, hover the cursor to the window you plan on sharing, and then click the **Share Window** button.

- Share all windows from an application: Click on the **App** button, hover the cursor to the window you plan on sharing, and then click on the **Share All[Application] Window** button
- Share multiple windows: While Sharing 1 or more windows, click the **Add Window** button. To stop sharing a window, simply click on the Remove icon in the window's preview.
- Share your screen: Click on the **Screen** button, hover the cursor to anywhere on your display, and then click on the **Share Screen** button.
- Change the window you are sharing: Hold the cursor over the shared window preview, click on the **Change Shared Window** button, hover the cursor to the window you'd like to share, and then click on the **Share This Window** button.

To stop sharing your display or a window, click on the Display Sharing button in the upper part of your screen, and then click on **Stop Sharing**.

Presenter Overlay

The Presenter Overlay feature makes it possible for other participants in the call to see you and then screen you are sharing at the same time. The big overlay places your shared screen beside you while you stay prominent so that you can move & talk in front of the screen. The small overlay puts your face in a bubble that can be moved around, so it's easy to see you while you showcase your work.

→ While on a FaceTime video call, click on the Video button 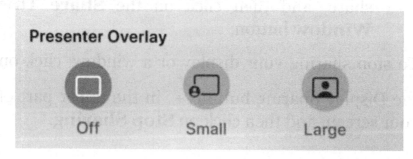 in the upper part of your display.

→ Pick any of the Presenter Overlay sizes. When start sharing your display, the overlay will appear immediately.

To disable Presenter Overlay, click on the Video icon in the upper part of your display, and then click the **Off** option under Presenter Overlay

Use video effects in FaceTime calls

Lists available video effects
for the selected camera.

Use video effects to place the focus on you or your reactions while making FaceTime video calls.

Use hand gestures to add reactions

You can use hand gestures to add reactions—visual effects that you use to express how you're feeling during a video call.

Choose one of the reactions below:

Reactions	Gestures	Icons

Fireworks		
Lasers		
Confetti		
Rain		
Balloons		
Thumbs down		
Thumbs up		
Hearts		

Note: When making use of hand gestures, hold your hands away from your face, and pause for a few seconds to activate the reaction effects.

To add reactions without using hand gestures, click the Video icon 🎦 in the upper part of your display, click the arrow ⌄ beside Reactions, and then click on any of the options. (If you cannot find the arrow, click on the **Reactions** button to activate the feature.)

To deactivate the Reactions feature, click the Video icon 🎦 in the upper part of your screen, and then click the **Reactions** button.

Use portrait mode

You can activate Portrait mode to automatically blur your background and place the visual focus on you.

While on a FaceTime video call, click on the Video icon 🎦 in the upper part of your screen, and then choose the **Portrait** option.

To change the background blur level, click on the arrow ⌄ beside Portrait, and then drag the slider.

To disable Portrait mode, click the Video icon ▭ in the upper part of your display, and then unselect Portrait.

Use Center Stage

Centre Stage keeps you and anybody close to you, centered in the frame as you move around while in the FaceTime video call.

While on a Face-Time video call, click on the Video icon ▭ in the upper part of your display, and then choose the **Centre Stage** option.

To disable Centre Stage, click on the Video icon ▭ in the upper part of your display, and then unselect Center Stage.

Use Studio Light

You can use Studio Light to darken the background and brighten your face.

While on a FaceTime video call, click on the Video icon ▭ in the upper part of your screen, and then choose the **Studio Light** option.

To change the background blur level, click on the arrow > beside Studio Light, and then drag the slider.

To disable Studio Light, click the Video icon in the upper part of your display, and then unselect Studio Light.

Capture Live Photos in a Face-Time call

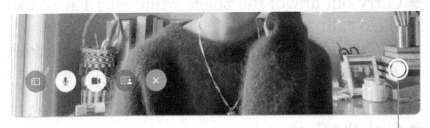

Live Photo button

You can capture Live Photos of a participant in a FaceTime video call. You and the participant will be notified that a picture was taken, and the picture will be stored in the Photos library.

Configure FaceTime for Live Photos

→ Launch the FaceTime application, click on **FaceTime** in the menu bar, click on **Settings** in the menu that appears, and then click the **General** button

➔ Tick the **Allow Live Photos to be captured in video calls** check box.

Setup the Photos application for Live Photos

Launch the Photos application 🌸 on your MacBook Air if you haven't already.

Capture Live Photos

➔ Carry out any of the below while on a Face-Time video call:
  ➢ On a single call: Select the Face-Time window.
  ➢ On a group call: Double-click the participant's tile.

➔ Click the Capture button ⚪.

Live Photo button

You can find the Live Photo in the Photos application.

Change audio options for FaceTime calls

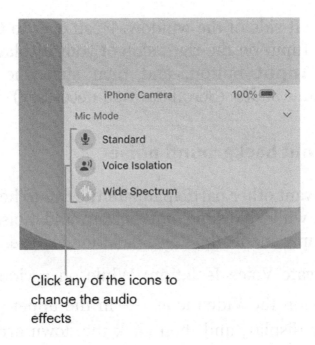

Click any of the icons to
change the audio
effects

Mute or change FaceTime call volume

Carry out any of the below while on a Face-Time call:

→ Mute your device: Hover the cursor over the call window, and then click on the Mute icon 🎤 .
Click on the icon once more to unmute your laptop.

→ Change the Microphone's volume: Click   on the Apple menu icon in the menu bar, click on the **System Settings** button in the menu, and then click on the **Sound** button in the sidebar on the left side of the window. Head over to Output and Input on the right side of your display, click the **Input** button, and then slide the Input Volume slider. (Scroll down, if necessary)

Filter out background noise

If you want other participants in the call to hear you clearly while blocking out background noise, you can simply enable the Voice Isolation feature.

→ Activate Voice Isolation: While on a video call, click on the Video icon ▣ in the upper part of your display, and then click the down arrow ∨ close to the Mic button ⬤ . Click on the right arrow › beside **Mic Mode**, and then choose the **Voice Isolation** option.

→ Enable the Voice Isolation feature in a voice call: While making a FaceTime voice call, click on the Audio icon ⬤ in the upper part of your display, and then choose the **Voice Isolation** option.

Add background sounds

If you want other participants in the call to hear your voice & the noise around you, you can simply enable the Wide Spectrum feature.

→ Activate Wide Spectrum: While on a FaceTime video call, click the Video icon ▢ in the upper part of your display, and then click on the down arrow ⌄ close to the MIC button 🎤. Click on the right arrow ⟩ beside **Mic Mode**, and then choose the **Wide Spectrum** button.

→ Activate the Wide Spectrum feature in a voice call: While making a FaceTime voice call, click on the Audio icon 🎤 in the upper part of your display, and then choose the **Wide Spectrum** option.

Use Live Captions

You can activate the Live Captions feature to see the conversation transcribed on your display during a FaceTime call.

→ While on a video call, click on the Sidebar icon ▦ to display the sidebar, and then click on the **Live Captions** button in the sidebar.

→ If prompted, click the **Download** button.

Deselect Live Captions in the side bar to deactivate this feature

Change FaceTime ringtones

➜ While using the FaceTime application, click on **FaceTime** in the menu bar, click on the **Settings** button in the menu that appears, and then click on the **General** button
➜ Click on the Ringtone drop-down menu, and then pick any of the ringtones.

Block callers on FaceTime

➜ While using the FaceTime application, click on **FaceTime** in the menu bar, click on Settings in the menu, and then click on Blocked.

➜ Click on the Add More icon ╈ , and then choose any of the names in your contacts list.
You can also block a caller from the recent calls list by simply Ctrl-clicking the contact, and then clicking on the **Block This Caller** button in the menu that appears.

To unblock a caller, click on **FaceTime** in the menu bar, click on Settings in the menu, and then click on the **Blocked** button. Choose any of the names in the list, and then click on the Remove icon ─ .

Delete your FaceTime call history

Carry out any of the below in the FaceTime application:

→ Delete a call: Ctrl-click on a call, and then click on the **Remove from Recents** button in the menu that appears.
→ Delete all recent calls: Click on **FaceTime** in the menu bar, and then click on the **Remove All Recents** button in the menu that appears.

CHAPTER 11

CONNECTIVITY WITH OTHER APPLE DEVICES

Unlock your MacBook Air & approve requests with your Apple Watch

You can use your Apple watch to unlock your MacBook or approve certain requests, without any need to insert a password.

Note: To use these features, ensure your Apple Watch is on your wrist and close to your laptop. Also, make sure both devices are making use of the same Apple ID, and 2-factor authentication is activated for your Apple ID.

Activate Auto Unlock and Approve with Apple Watch

➔ Click the Apple menu icon in the menu bar, click on the **System Settings** button in the menu that appears, and then click on Touch ID & Passcode in the sidebar on the left side of the window.

→ Head over to Apple Watch on the right side of the window, and then enable the option close to your Apple watch's name.
This feature is only available for Apple Watches using watchOS or after

Unlock your MacBook

Open the lid or press any of the keys on your keyboard to wake your MacBook from its idle state. The screen will indicate that your laptop has been unlocked.

Approve apps requests

Double-click your watch's side button to approve requests from your MacBook Air

Whenever an application requires authentication on your MacBook, an approval request from your device will appear on your smartwatch; simply double-press your watch's side button to approve the request.

Use your iPhone as a webcam on your MacBook Air

The **Continuity Camera** feature allows you to use your iPhone as your MacBook's microphone or webcam, and take advantage of your iPhone's video effects.

Getting Started

Before using the Continuity Camera setting, you must:

→ Ensure your MacBook Air is running macOS 13 or after and the iPhone is using iOS 16 or after.

- ➔ Ensure you're using the same Apple ID on both devices and 2-factor authentication is activated for your Apple ID.
- ➔ Activate Bluetooth & WiFi on your MacBook Air and iPhone
- ➔ Mount your iPhone: Your iPhone must be near your MacBook Air, Locked, Stable, & positioned with its back camera facing you without any obstruction

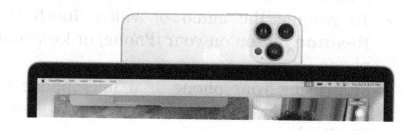

Use your iPhone as a microphone or webcam

- ➔ Open any app on your MacBook Air that can access the microphone or camera, such as Face-Time or Photos Booth.
- ➔ In the application's menu bar or setting, pick your iPhone as the microphone or camera. (For instance, when using the FaceTime app, click on the **Video** button in the menu bar, and then select your iPhone as the camera. Or, when using the Photos Booth application, click the **Camera**

button in the upper part of your display, and then choose your iPhone as the camera.)

The Continuity application will open on your iPhone and start streaming video or audio from the back camera to your laptop.

→ Carry out any of the below:

- To pause the audio or video, simply touch the Pause button on your iPhone or unlock your phone.

- To resume the audio or video, touch the **Resume** button on your iPhone, or lock your phone.

- Stop using your phone as a microphone or webcam: Exit the application on your MacBook.

- Remove your phone as an option: Touch the **Disconnect** button on your iPhone, and confirm that you want to disconnect.
  To reconnect your iPhone, simply use a USB cable to connect your phone to your MacBook Air.

Automatically switch to your iPhone's camera

Your MacBook can automatically use your iPhone as its camera for some Mac applications, such as

Photos Booth & Face-Time. To do this, your iPhone must:

→ Be near your MacBook
→ Be in landscape orientation
→ Have its back camera facing you without any obstructions
→ Be stationary
→ Not be lying flat
→ Have its screen off.

If you have used your phone as a webcam on your MacBook before, other applications on your laptop might also remember your iPhone as your preferred camera.

Make your iPhone the default microphone

You can turn your iPhone into the primary microphone for your MacBook.

→ Click the Apple menu icon in the menu bar, click on **System Settings** in the menu, and then click the **Sound** button in the sidebar on the left side of the window. (Scroll down, if necessary.)
→ Choose your phone from the sound input devices list.
The Continuity application will open on your iPhone & start capturing sound.

If your iPhone does not appear as a microphone or camera option

If you can't find your iPhone in the microphone or camera list in the Sound or application settings, try the following:

→ Use a USB cable to connect your phone to your MacBook and recheck. (If it is already connected by cable, disconnect and reconnect.)
→ Make sure of the following:
  • You are using an iPhone XR or after.
  • Your MacBook Air is using macOS 13.0 or after.
  • Your iPhone is using iOS 16.0 or after.
  • Your iPhone has the Continuity Camera feature activated in the Settings app> General> AirPlay & Handoff.
  • Your iPhone accepts your MacBook as a trusted device.
  • Both your iPhone & MacBook have Bluetooth, WiFi, and two-factor authentication activated.
  • Both devices are using the same Apple ID
  • Both devices are within 30ft of each other.
  • Your iPhone is not sharing its mobile connection, and your MacBook is not sharing its internet connection.

- Your chosen video application has been updated to the most recent version.

Continuity Camera

The Continuity Camera feature allows you can take a photo or scan a document with an iPad or iPhone's camera and have the picture or scanned document instantly appear on your MacBook air, just where you want it to be—for instance, in a folder, note, e-mail, or document.

Before using the Continuity Camera setting, you must:

➜ Ensure your MacBook, iPad, & iPhone are using the latest version of macOS, iPadOS, & iOS.
➜ Ensure you're using the same Apple ID on both devices and 2-factor authentication is activated for your Apple ID.
➜ Activate Bluetooth & WiFi on your MacBook Air and iPhone

Adhere to the directives below to use the Continuity Camera feature:

➜ Place the cursor where you want to insert the scanned document or picture on your MacBook Air.

For instance, in an e-mail, note, or document

→ Click on the **File** button, click on **Insert from iPad or iPhone** in the menu that appears, and then click on Scan Documents or Take Photo.

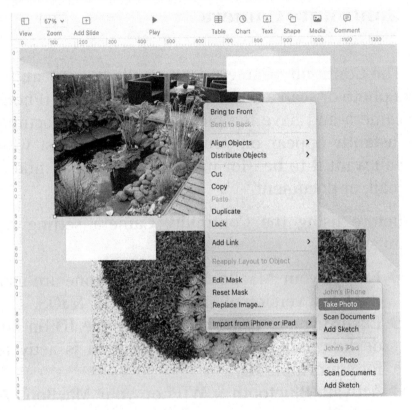

In some applications, you can click on **File** in the menu bar, click on the **Import from iPad or iPhone** button in the menu that appears, and click on Take Photos or Scan Document to create a new file with scans or pictures. You can also Ctrl-click your Mac's desktop or a folder in a Finder window, click on **Import from iPad or**

iPhone, and then click on Scan Document or Take Photos.

If the commands are not available in the File menu, they may be in a different menu (like the Insert or Edit menu), or the application you are using may not be compatible with Continuity Camera.

→ Do any of the below on your iPad or iPhone:

- For a scan: Scan the document. Your iPad or iPhone will detect the edges of the document and automatically adjust the area covered— if you want to manually adjust the edges, simply drag the frame. When you are done, click on the **Keep Scan** button or the **Retake** button.

- For a picture: Capture the picture, and then touch the **Use Photo or Retake** button.

➔ The scanned document or photo will appear where you placed the cursor on your MacBook Air, or as a file if you started from a folder or the desktop.

Handoff

The Handoff feature allows you to start something on one Apple device and pick it up on another Apple device seamlessly. For instance, you can start replying to an e-mail on your iPad, and finish the e-mail in the Mail application on your MacBook Air. The Handoff feature is compatible with many Apple applications, like Safari, Pages, Contacts, etc. Some 3rd party applications might also work with the Handoff feature.

To use the **Handoff** feature, you must activate Handoff, Bluetooth, & WiFi on your MacBook, iPad & iPhone. You must also sign in with the same Apple ID on both Apple devices.

Enable or turn off Handoff

→ On your MacBook: Click the Apple menu icon🍎 in the menu bar, click on the **System Settings** button in the menu, and then click on General in the sidebar on the left side of the window. Click on AirDrop & Handoff on the right side of the window, and then activate or deactivate "**Allow Handoff between this Mac & your iCloud devices**"

→ On iPad or iPhone: Navigate to the Settings app, click General, touch AirPlay & Handoff, and then enable or disable **Hand-off**.

→ On your Apple Watch: Launch the Apple Watch application on your iPhone, tap the **My Watch** tab, tap General, and then enable or deactivate the **Enable Handoff** feature.

Hand off between devices

→ From your MacBook to an iPad or iPhone: The Handoff icon of the application you are making use of on your MacBook Air will appear at the end of the Dock on your iPad or at the bottom of the Apps Switcher screen on your iPhone. Touch the button to continue working in the application.

→ From an iPad, iPhone, or Apple Watch to your MacBook Air: The Handoff icon of the application you are using on your Apple Watch, iPad, or iPhone will appear close to the right end of the Dock on your MacBook Air. Click on the icon to continue using the application.

You can also press Command-Tab to switch to the application that has the Handoff icon.

Universal Clipboard

The **Universal Clipboard** feature allows you to copy videos, pictures, & text on an Apple device and then paste them on another Apple device. For instance, you can copy text from your MacBook Air and paste it into a document on your nearby iPad. Or copy files from an iMac to paste into a folder on your MacBook.

To use the **Universal Clipboard** feature, you must enable Handoff, Bluetooth, & WiFi on your MacBook, iPad & iPhone. You must also log in with the same Apple ID on both Apple devices.

Enable or deactivate Handoff

→ On your MacBook: Click the Apple menu icon in the menu bar, click on the **System Settings** button in the menu, and then click on General in the sidebar on the left side of the window. Click on AirDrop & Handoff on the right side of the window, and then activate or deactivate "**Allow Handoff between this Mac & your iCloud devices**"

→ On iPad or iPhone: Navigate to the Settings app, click General, touch AirPlay & Handoff, and then enable or disable **Hand-off**.

→ On your Apple Watch: Launch the Apple Watch application on your iPhone, tap the **My Watch** tab, tap General, and then enable or deactivate the **Enable Handoff** feature.

Follow the directives below to use the Universal Clipboard feature:

→ Copy on a device: Select the content you'd like to copy, and then copy it. For example, on your MacBook Air, press the Command-C keyboard combination or click on the **Edit** button, and then click on the **Copy** button in the menu that appears.

Any content you copy should be pasted as soon as possible

→ Paste on a device: Place the cursor where you want to paste the content, and then paste the content. For instance, on your iPhone, double-tap, and then touch the **Paste** button in the menu that appears.

INDEX

Split View, 100, 101, 102, 104

Spotlight, 21, 23, 24, 38, 63, 64, 65, 156, 160

Stage Manager, 53, 112, 113, 114, 115, 116, 117, 118

storage, 4, 70, 144, 145, 161, 162, 163, 164

Studio Light, 218

T

Touch ID, 3, 5, 12, 18, 19, 89, 90, 91, 92, 93, 188, 204, 226

trackpad, 13, 26, 27, 32, 34, 36, 37, 49, 58, 88, 100, 122, 136, 198

Trackpad, 17, 26, 27, 28, 32, 33

Translate, 140, 178, 181

U

Universal Clipboard, 238, 239

USB, 3, 33, 34, 35, 77, 230, 232

USB-C, 3

User, 143

V

Voice Isolation, 222

volume, 83, 84, 85, 221

Volume, 21, 222

W

wallpaper, 38, 105, 106, 107, 118

webcam, 228, 229, 230, 231

Wide Spectrum, 222, 223

widgets, 47, 52

WiFi, 8, 38, 54, 76, 77, 229, 232, 233, 236, 238

Made in the USA
Middletown, DE
02 September 2024